Sisters

Sisters

The Story Goes On

Janice Chaffee

FOREWORD BY GLORIA GAITHER

Thomas Nelson Publishers
Nashville • Atlanta • London • Vancouver

Published in Nashville, Tennessee, by Thomas Nelson, Inc., Publishers, and distributed in Canada by Word Communications, Ltd., Richmond, British Columbia, and in the United Kingdom by Word (UK), Ltd., Milton Keynes, England.

Unless otherwise noted, Scripture quotations are taken from the HOLY BIBLE, NEW INTERNATIONAL VERSION®. Copyright © 1973, 1978, 1984 by International Bible Society. Used by permission of Zondervan Bible Publishing House. All rights reserved.

The "NIV" and "New International Version" trademarks are registered in the United States Patent and Trademark Office by International Bible Society. Use of either trademark requires the permission of International Bible Society.

Scripture quotations noted NKJV are from THE NEW KING JAMES VERSION. Copyright © 1979, 1980, 1982, 1990, 1994, Thomas Nelson, Inc., Publishers.

Scripture quotations noted NRSV are from the NEW REVISED STANDARD VERSION of the Bible © 1989 by the Division of Christian Education of the National Council of the Churches of Christ in the U.S.A. All rights reserved.

All lyric quotes are from songs featured on the albums *Sisters* and *Sisters: The Story Goes On*, Warner Alliance. Lyric from "Broken Places" is featured on the album *Human Song*, Myrrh Records.

Library of Congress Cataloging-in-Publication Data

Chaffee, Janice.
  Sisters : the story goes on / Janice Chaffee.
    p. cm.
  Includes bibliographical references.
  ISBN 0-7852-7601-7
  1. Christian women—United States—Biography. 2. Women—
Religious life. 3. Christian life. 4. Gospel musicians—United States—
Biography. I. Title.
BR1713.C39 1995
248.8′43—dc20   95-4494
                                                                       CIP

Printed in the United States of America

2 3 4 5 6 7 — 02 01 00 99 98 97 96

For the women who love me
as a sister

Contents

FOREWORD

She was the voice on the telephone that said she'd be over to watch my babies so I could have a few moments to myself to restore my soul and rest my weary body.

She was the one who sent the handwritten note to tell me she'd be there praying for me when I delivered the address at the Governor's Prayer Breakfast.

Hers were the arms that held me as I sobbed out my grief when cancer took my mother's final breath, and she passed into a place I could not yet see or go to.

She was the one who came week after week to help clean my house when the load of my commitments and the demands of my calling were more than I could handle alone.

She fixed me soup and put me to bed when I was recovering from surgery.

She sent me silly cards that made me laugh and "kidnapped" me from overwork to shop or walk by the creek or simply sip lemonade on the porch.

She critiqued my writing, ignored my failures, insisted I could when I thought I couldn't, and believed in me when

I wanted to quit. She prayed for me when I was too weak to pray for myself, and she celebrated my successes.

She wore many different faces—old, middle-aged, and young—and she came from a variety of backgrounds. She was my mother, my daughter, my sibling, my neighbor, my pastor, my student, my teacher, my mentor, my new acquaintance, and my longtime friend. But always my sister in the Lord, sent to help me see God's presence in the nitty-gritty of my days.

I believe it was God's intention that we be ministering siblings to each other, for Jesus said to his friends: "I have loved you like I have so that you can see how the Father loves Me. Now, you love each other like this." On His last night with them, after they had eaten together, He encouraged them, prayed for them, told them eternal secrets, and washed their feet. Afterward, from that place of community, He walked with them to Gethsemane and from there He walked alone to the cross, where He would redeem His friends. "I call you not servants," He said, "but friends."

Sisters is a collection of personal stories told by women and by agents of healing who took seriously Christ's mandate to be a friend in times of brokenness, despair, failure, or exaltation. It is an honest book of forgiveness, joy, and reconciliation. It is a testament to the healing power of love.

This collection is the work of my sister in the Lord, Janice Chaffee. It accompanies two wonderful recording projects that Janice created with Gail Hamilton and Cheryl Rogers. These three sisters, all dear to my life and pilgrimage, brought together women who, in many styles of music, share their love for God and a life of communicating the gospel.

It is not surprising that Solomon in the Song of Songs

calls the soul "sister." We artists who joined our hearts and voices to record those projects, and those women who share their stories in this book, are not surprised by Solomon's sweet word. In the body of Christ, sisters are more than mere siblings; they are soul mates.

May you feel the harmony of sisterhood in your soul as you read these stories. May women everywhere be sensitized to become not only agents of healing and mercy in a broken world but eager celebrants of one another's accomplishments, victories, and joys!

Gloria Gaither

Acknowledgments

Grateful acknowledgment is given to Thomas Nelson Publishers, especially to Ken Stephens, for remaining committed and enthusiastic; to Lonnie Hull DuPont, for her encouragement and kindness; and to Holly Halverson, for her assistance and friendship.

I am thankful for Gail Hamilton and Cheryl Rogers, my sisters not only in recording albums, but in my everyday life. We truly are sisters in the Lord.

Barbara Pine edited my writing, guided my words, and celebrated my progress. I am indebted to her influence and thankful for her friendship.

INTRODUCTION

What happens when a true story is told? A picture unfolds. The teller chooses how much to tell, and whether the telling is brief or wordy, it carries important elements. A teller divulges information, she risks reactions, she attempts to be understood. A storyteller uses words to represent realities—like attitudes, needs, intentions—that cannot otherwise be apprehended.

What happens when a true story is heard? The listener processes information, chooses reactions, perceives the feeling behind the storyteller's words. She has the privilege of interpretation. A good listener, if wise, learns from what she hears and incorporates this newfound knowledge into her own life.

Every woman has a story to tell. And every woman has a story to hear. Our personal lives cannot remain entirely private. In sisterhood, women must merge voices. Sometimes we tell and sometimes we listen. We share our pain, and we share our healing, our overcoming, our comfort, as lavishly as we received it. First a recipient, then a deliverer:

Praise be to the God and Father of our Lord Jesus Christ, the Father of compassion and the God of all comfort, who comforts us in all our troubles, so that we can comfort those in any trouble with the comfort we ourselves have received from God (2 Cor. 1:3–4).

Some stories are still in progress. Beginnings are before us, clearly, but the end may or may not be in sight. Sisters seldom relate to one another on the basis of completed stories. Seldom do we get to make perfect responses. We are not responsible for or required to agree with a sister's behavior, actions, or choices. We *are* called to remain in relationship with our sister, to walk next to her, and to offer our strength and support.

Here is a story of mine. In the first session of a women's retreat, I opened with a brief summary of my past year. I knew many of the women gathered there with me, so I was tempted to gloss over the hassles of our recent move from one state to another, but I could not. These women were my friends, and they deserved the truth from me.

Instead of omitting it, I admitted that my husband's recent job transfer to Colorado and our transition from California were hard. I confessed my frustration with the relocation, feeling anger when the dry cleaner shrunk my only wool jacket, unfolding and refolding maps, trying to grasp the layout of the city, and sliding across the ice through an intersection and sheepishly waving to applauding drivers in safely stopped cars. I was convinced that my California license plates flashed inexperience like neon signs. I dreaded having to visit churches, search for familiar name brands in the local grocery store, open new bank accounts and apply for ATM cards, and remember new phone numbers. I hated holding my son while he cried, "I want to go home."

I admitted, too, that in spite of the inconveniences and nuisances, I had peace. My husband Jim and I ardently believed that the Lord directed our move. That we *belonged* in Colorado did not diminish our frustrations but did put them in perspective. And, in spite of the tensions, we had a sense of belonging and purpose in our new home. We made an effort to counterbalance the more noticeable hassles with the less visible confidence of a good move.

To the women in that room, I told the truth, and unexpectedly, my honesty set the tone—this was a safe place to confess inner weaknesses and failings.

One by one, my friends stood and spoke. They were frank, transparent, and emotional. Their personal pain was no longer private. Many precious and sensitive issues now belonged to us all.

Carol, from Florida, stood. "Yes," she whispered, pointing to her head and giggling self-consciously. "This is a wig. I had a mastectomy six weeks ago, and I knew if I could just live until I got here, I would find help. If you have had this kind of surgery, please come talk with me."

Eleanor, forthright and vibrant as always, truthfully revealed, "I'm in love with my husband again. Some of you know it's been rough for a few years. I've *liked* him during this time, but now I can honestly say I *love* him."

Judy, usually lighthearted and humorous, stood, wept, and said, "It's been more than ten years since our son died, but the pain sometimes is still overwhelming. And it hurt when a friend said to me, 'Aren't you over that yet?' "

Terri, a vibrant, single, career woman, stood silent for several minutes as tears and pain choked her voice. "I hate God. He's just like the dad who always promises to take you to Disneyland but never does. I've been a good girl; I've kept my end of the bargain. Where is my husband? Where are my children? When do I get the desire of my heart?"

So great was their need for comfort that these women exposed their deepest feelings. They bravely revealed their innermost selves; they risked criticism, judgment, embarrassment, and rejection.

Shortly after the meeting, I looked around the room. I saw five or six women crowded about Carol, hugging and laughing. Others clustered around Eleanor, celebrating her renewed love for her husband. Terri listened intently to the counsel from women surrounding her. Friends held Judy as she wept. The responses came out of compassion and experience. Solace was given because they knew what words and actions would be most comforting or because their love compelled them to give comfort. These women lovingly knew how to "carry each other's burdens" (Gal. 6:2).

This is true sisterhood, I thought. Women of faith, loving each other, guiding each other, laughing and crying with each other through good times and bad.

However, not everyone feels as free as these women to confess private feelings. What makes us hesitate? What causes our insecurity, our reluctance to ask for help? Or, how do we react when someone actually admits her problems to us?

Do we withdraw emotionally, not wanting to get involved in another's problem?

Ideally, when we enter Christian sisterhood, we come in the name of Jesus, in the name of that One who does not abandon or betray. As surely as Mary and Martha were sisters, they were individuals. So are we. As surely as they were individuals, they managed to misunderstand and frustrate one another. So can we. The goal of Christian sisterhood is not conformity, but faithfulness. The basis is God's goodness, not the guarantee of our own. The proof of sisterhood comes when trust is great enough among us that we share our stories.

This book contains my story and the stories of many other women. Sometimes the sister tells her own story, sometimes I tell it for her, and sometimes we tell it together. Some stories are told with laughter, some with tears. Some of the names you may recognize, some you may not. Some names have been changed for the sake of children or for protection. The tellers represent various ages, races, and denominations; they are single, married, and divorced. Their stories are told to encourage you, to teach you, and to prepare you for having and being a sister. They are meant for hope if you are in the same situation, for learning how to help another who needs your comfort and strength.

Each story needs to be read with two questions in the reader's mind. One, "What would I have done in that situation?" Two, "What will I do if I have an opportunity to help a sister in that situation?"

I am grateful to women whose lives are courageously lent to this book. Though some of the stories seem too complex or startling to be true, I assure you that each is. The experiences of these stories are not limited to the women gathered here. They live in the women who sit next to you in the pew, who live across the street, who work in your office. They may be in your family; one may be yours.

Sisters

I've never walked a mile in your shoes
Tasted the tears you've cried
I've never known the deepest longings
You hold inside

But I've had my share of disenchantments
Days when I've been so low
And I'm here to say no matter the heartache
You're not alone

I will be there with you
through all the joy and sorrow
I will be there to point you to the One
who holds each tomorrow

Chorus:
We are sisters, sisters in the Lord
Our faith in common, sisters in the Lord
No matter how the world defines us
Nothing can break the tie that binds us
We are sisters, in the Lord

We were all little girls at one time
Full of hopes and dreams
And now as we give ourselves we're learning
What love really means

I will be there with you
through all the joy and sorrow
I will be there to point you to the One
who holds each tomorrow

Take my hand
I'll take yours
We'll reach together
For the hand of our Lord

Chorus:
We are sisters, sisters in the Lord
Our faith in common, sisters in the Lord
No matter how the world defines us
Nothing can break the tie that binds us
We are sisters, in the Lord[1]

1

Motherhood:
Is There a Right Way?

---

*"Finally I heard the liberating truth:
I did not have to be like
other mothers."*

I recently attended a women's conference in Seattle. I met my assigned roommate, Elaine, and we proceeded to acquaint ourselves with each other. I told her I produced record albums and was in the process of writing a book. She told me she was a business consultant for software companies. She was married, she said, and the mother of two sons, as I am. As we talked about our children, I admitted, "I love my boys, but I'm not a very good mother."

Elaine's mouth flew open, and she stared at me. I felt an urgent need to clarify what I had just said. "I'm not a *natural* mom," I explained. "I have to work really hard at my 'mothering.'"

Elaine responded by saying, "I've never heard a woman admit that before. I feel the same way."

Our conversation took off. We realized that we both hoped to "mother" well, but for us, that does not come easily or naturally.

In another conversation, I told an acquaintance that the book I was writing was for women, and she immediately asked, "Will you write about women who work versus women who stay at home?"

"Why?" I asked.

"Because," she replied, "I feel so put down because I stay at home and am 'just a mom.'"

I laughed. When I was a working mother, I felt put down because I *didn't* stay at home. Is staying at home or working outside the home a true measure of a *good* mother?

My Story

A few months after my son Elliott was born, I returned to work. I was determined not to let his presence disrupt my preestablished lifestyle. But I quickly discovered I had not factored into the equation my love for him and my desire to spend time with him. A conflict arose: I wanted to pursue my career, and I wanted to be a good mom. But my skills at work were more refined than my skills as a mother. Before long, pressure from work went home with me and guilt from leaving my son traveled to work. During the first year of Elliott's life, the few hours I had with him in the morning and evening were not as fulfilling as I had hoped. It was Pati, Elliott's caregiver, who taught me maternal skills.

Pati kissed and hugged and loved Elliott with the same affection she showed her own son Jacob, who is one day younger than Elliott. What a pair these boys were! Chubby, fair, blue-eyed Elliott propped up next to wiry, olive-skinned, black-haired Jacob. Elliott loved going to Pati's house, which was always happy, if not always spotless. Pati read to the boys, taught them songs about Jesus, made wonderful treats. Meals and snack times began with little hands tightly clasped, eyes squished shut. Lisping voices echoed Pati's prayer, concluding with a loud "amen!" Every argument over a toy, every cut knee, every sullen attitude was tended with a prayer or a lesson about God. Even now, Elliott and I recall the image of Pati rocking in her chair, open Bible in her lap, reading the Word that was clearly precious to her. Each day, Pati's most important goal was to teach Jacob and Elliott just how much they were loved by God and herself. I was not jealous of Pati or the love Elliott had for her. I was filled with awe.

What a pair Pati and I were. My schedule was frantic: I tried to cram career, marriage, and parenting into every twenty-four-hour day. My house was loud and raucous; her house was calm and peaceful. I had a list of things I had to accomplish each day; Pati's main accomplishment was to love the boys and expand their awareness of self, of God, and of each other. I was awkward as a parent; she was a natural.

Pati's contentment grew by being at home, loving Jacob. Her son was very precious and for five reasons: Pati had suffered loss of three miscarriages, her son John lived one day, and her daughter Billie lived one month. "When the doctors told me that my son was not going to make it, and when they told me it was hopeless for Billie, and when they told me not to risk getting pregnant again, I still had the hope of being a mother. I believed that God is able to do immeasurably more than all we ask or imagine (Eph. 3:20). When he gave me more than I dared to dream—Jacob Joseph, my healthy, strong son—it seemed almost unbelievable."

Then, according to Pati, God gave her another child to love, my son Elliott. Now she had two boys to guide, to teach, to feed, and to love. As thoroughly as Pati believes God added Elliott to her life, I believe God added Pati to my life. When time permitted at the end of my workday, I stayed in her company for hours, watching how she responded to the boys, joked with them, and played. I watched her drop a load of laundry on the couch, warm from the dryer, and then drop the boys in the middle of the pile. The toddlers "helped" fold the clothes. Sometimes when I arrived, Pati and the boys were on the floor, putting a puzzle together. Sometimes they were in the kitchen cooking. Sometimes they waded in the little plastic pool, naked—the boys, not Pati!

When our son Taylor was born nearly two years later, I decided to stay at home and give full-time mothering a try. I don't know if Elliott or I missed Pati more. My feelings of failure escalated. Even though I *chose* to leave the office and enter the workplace called home, the adjustment was difficult. I was at a loss. How *does* one make edible Play-doh in six different cholesterol-free, nontoxic colors? I couldn't build an elaborate tree house out of scrap lumber like my friend Vickie did for her children. Nor could I transform children's bedrooms into castles or spaceships with two cans of paint

and three yards of fabric, like my friend Bridgett. I was paralyzed. I did not know how to be creative with my sons. I
did not know how to spontaneously enjoy them, like Pati.
I couldn't even make grilled cheese sandwiches the right way.
"Pati doesn't make them that way," Elliott authoritatively
announced.

Staying at home with an infant and a two-year-old did not
require the same skills or fit the pace of the office. If only
my boys needed management, rather than attentive care. My
previous job had allowed me to organize, delegate, process,
route, prepare, advertise, schedule, edit, balance, and super-
vise an entire division. I loved the pressure of the deadlines,
the schmoozing on the telephone, the authority. Peanut
butter on celery was not my idea of a great power lunch.
Reading Bert and Ernie books paled in comparison to inter-
office communication. Folding laundry, washing dishes, and
vacuuming floors failed to provide the sense of accomplishment I had felt tackling projects at the office. Where was
Pati's joy, Pati's fulfillment? Work at home was never complete. The chore I finished one day needed attention the very
next day. Guilt for missing the office replaced the guilt I had
felt for not staying at home! As a mother, I felt failure. I
needed a fresh view.

In my desire to be a good mother, I inflicted the curse of
shoulds on myself. I should be more like Pati. I should read
more books to the boys. I should sign them up for gymnas-
tics. I should buy little games to stimulate their intelligence.
Maybe Elliott should go to a private nursery school for a few
days a week. Perhaps Taylor and I should join a mother-child
aerobics class. I felt I should maintain a picture-perfect house.

These issues became demands rather than options. Achieving these goals would be admirable, but not essential. My concern for the *appearances* and *shoulds* of good mothering took more energy than the actuality of good mothering. *Doing* buried *being*.

As if all my insecurities of good mothering were not enough, I also felt extreme guilt over my lack of Bible study and prayer. Never mind that demands for my time began at dawn and stretched far into the night. No wonder my attempts to read the Bible often put me to sleep. How humorous it is to recall that one of the great lessons I learned about mothering came from a former priest! In a conversation about prayer with my friend Brennan Manning, he gently assured me, saying, "This is a season to meditate, to reflect on the Scriptures you already have memorized. Pray for your son as you nurse him. Be honest with God. Say to Him, 'I'm tired. Know that I love You. Thank You for this child. *Please* let us sleep tonight.'"

Richard Foster also frees mothers from self-inflicted guilt:

The demands that your baby makes are immense. The interruptions never end. Also, your sleep is seldom deep because you always have one ear open for your baby. It is important to recognize this fact and be easy with yourself. This time will pass—sooner than you think. Rather than trying to pray in some fanciful isolation that you will never find, discover God in your times with your baby. God will become real to you through your baby. The times of play with your baby *are* your prayer. You may be able to pray during feeding time—this is especially true for nursing mothers—so sing your prayers to the Lord. In a few short months you will be able to return to a more regular pattern of prayer.[2]

I poured out my frustration to an older friend. Instead of feeling sorry for me or offering immediate words of wisdom, she let loose a hearty laugh. I was surprised by her seemingly insensitive response. Still chuckling, she said, "You had a job that would drive most people crazy. Now stop trying to live up to a preconceived idea of what a 'good mother' is. Apply your God-given abilities and the skills you developed in your career to your role as a mother."

Her simple words were freeing. Finally, I heard the liberating truth. I did not have to be like other mothers. I could learn from them, but that did not require mimicking them. My problems came into focus: Comparing my new mothering duties to an old reference point didn't work. I might well apply my skills to being a parent, but I could not map my progress as a mother the way I could monitor progress in the office. Short-term tasks could not be compared to the long-term task of parenting. When I changed my perspective, I started to enjoy my days with the boys. I learned to see my sons as people, not projects.

Pati helped me develop as a good mother. She taught me the importance of *loving* the boys rather than *doing* specific things with the boys. Just because she did things a certain way did not mean that I had to. Elliott, Taylor, and I often met Pati and her sons Jacob and Matthew at the park. Sometimes Pati entrusted me with the privilege of keeping all four boys for a few hours! After I learned to relax, I enjoyed myself.

The Story Goes On

Many mothers I talk to confess feelings of guilt, tiredness, and frustration. For some, these feelings are fleeting. For others, like me, it takes a good while to overcome them. For example, Jean, the mother of a six-month-old son, asked, "You know the bonding you read about? When does that happen?"

Dianne, on her fortieth birthday, confessed, "I am tired, really tired, of chasing a two-year-old and nursing an infant. How will I feel in another few years? How will I cope when I get older?"

Lisa and her husband were living in a new town, struggling financially, and adjusting to both married life and parenthood. As if this weren't enough stress, Lisa unintentionally set their apartment on fire. "I simply forgot to turn off the stove. Leaving the house, I forgot about the bottles sterilizing in a pan of boiling water. When I came home, fire trucks surrounded what was left of our apartment building. I felt so guilty. There was no denying it was my fault."

Ah, the peaceful pace of motherhood!

Debbie resented her baby because she lost independence. She missed the freedom to make choices that now seemed selfish. Her previous job had helped shape a strong identity and cultivate self-esteem. Her new job of mother seemed foreign and scary. Eventually, she learned to balance identity with motherhood without lessening either.

Lest I paint only a bleak picture of motherhood, I hasten to add that my friend Karen believes there is no greater work on earth than to sit on the floor and play with her daughter and son. "At first, I thought I *had* to sit on the floor," she admits. "But now I *want* to sit there and play with them. I want them to know that our lives are connected. They help me make beds, and I praise them for their efforts. When they say, 'It's time to wrestle, Mom,' I get down and wrestle with them. I do it because I see that our future together requires my staying well connected with the present. They need to actively hear, see, touch, and experience life *with* me. I want to leave a legacy. I want them to follow after me as I follow after Christ. Nothing could please me more than for my children to recognize God's voice and say, 'That sounds a lot like Mom.' I take seriously the job of mirroring God's love and of developing godly behavior."

Dr. Ann Dally speaks for Karen and most mothers when she states, "Children need loving care. . . . Children are not born with vices that must be eradicated and controlled, but with personalities that need to be developed by good mothering and child care and by happy family life."[3]

When my neighbor, Catherine, became a new mom, she went to other mothers for advice. She learned "We are to teach our children how to accept love; this enables them to accept God's most loving gift of His son, Jesus Christ. And we are to teach our children how to give that love to others; this teaches them the Christian's life of service and witness. Psalm 127:3 teaches me that children are valuable: 'Children [are] a reward from Him.'"

Cindy knows this and adores being at home with her children. She especially loves unexpected snow days "when we put everything aside and play games all day, pop popcorn, and make gingerbread men. If one of the children is sick, I welcome the gift of attention I can give him." Cindy loves to plan walks to the park, bicycle rides, and picnics. She spends hours in the car, driving her three boys to karate, basketball, baseball, and soccer. "What a great honor and responsibility it is for me to teach them about all kinds of things, but especially about the Lord. I feel free to nurture them because I know how God has nurtured me. I can fall into His arms in my darkest time and He holds me through everything. I want to model that reality to my children."

All the mothers I talk to, whether they work inside or outside the home, stress the need for time alone and the healthy addition of their own interests and activities to their day. They all mentioned the value of time spent with other mothers of children the same ages. Cindy joined a local chapter of MOPS (Mothers of Preschoolers) for encouragement. She is convinced that she is a better mother, wife, and friend because she continues to play the flute and takes gourmet cooking classes. Karen has a part-time color and fashion consultation business. Dianne sells cosmetics in home showings.

Remembering and writing about Pati and her influence in my life prompted me to call her. We laughed and cried as we reminisced about our years of friendship. I thanked her for all she taught me and what she did for me. "Thank *you* for what you did for me," she countered.

"What on earth did I do for you?" I asked.

"You trusted me with your child," she replied. "When I looked at you and saw your organization and determination and confidence, I knew I wasn't able to do your job. But your trust made me realize that I was good at different things. And you appreciated what I did. You trusted me with Elliott's care; you trusted me with your feelings and allowed us to cry together. You trusted my relationship with God and my faith. Your belief and trust in me built me up and made me feel like a better person. You allowed me the privilege of loving your son. And of loving you."

Is there a right way to be a mother? Yes. To try and do the best we can. Kathy homeschools her daughter. Sue sends her children to private Christian schools. My kids go to the local public school. We all dearly love our children and want them to receive a good education. Same goal, only different methods.

Is there a right way to pray as a mom? Yes. Anywhere, any place, any time. Pati reads her Bible early in the morning before the children wake up and during their naps. I read my Bible at night. God hears our prayers, whether offered from a church pew on a Sunday morning or from a rocking chair in the middle of the night. When our toddlers race up to us, we give them a quick hug and kiss, and off they run again. If we are truly God's children, He understands our racing needs, our quick prayers, and He responds as we do with our own children.

Is there a right way to raise our children? Yes. Together. Some women choose to or must maintain their employment outside the home. Some mothers choose to or enjoy staying at home. Both types of mother work on behalf of their children. And like Pati and me, they can learn from each other.

Elliott and Taylor are now ages eleven and nine, and still I am not a natural mother. I constantly watch how other mothers interact with their children. I listen to the patience in their voices. I see them diffuse a tense situation with humor. I watch them respond to their children firmly, but calmly. I make mental notes: *I can try that.*

But, even with the lack of a natural ability, I passionately love my sons. Every night before they go to sleep, I remind them of that. "Never forget," I tell them.

"How can we?" they reply, sometimes with annoyance, sometimes with a smile. "You tell us all the time."

Good, I think to myself. *I've done something right.*

How great is the love the Father has lavished on us, that we should be called children of God! And that is what we are!

1 JOHN 3:1

2

Single Mothers:
Don't Miss
the Miracle

---

*"Life breaks us all sometimes in
unexpected ways and some of us grow
strong in the broken places."*
Ernest Hemingway

A realtor stuck a For Sale sign in the grass of our front yard a few days after Christmas. That same day, my husband Jim loaded his car with most of his clothes and drove away to begin a new job in another state. That same day, I became, temporarily, a single mom.

At first, it was kind of fun. I had the bathroom to myself, and the bedroom stayed relatively picked up. I could read in bed late into the night without bothering Jim.

Every two or three weeks, Jim returned for a weekend.

The boys were delighted to see him, to show him school papers, to tell him about baseball games, to wrestle on the living room floor. I, too, was delighted to see him, but for decidedly different reasons. When he was home, I handed him all the decision-making responsibilities. I did not care what, when, or where we ate. It did not matter to me when we got up, where we went, what our activities were. I just did not want to make a decision.

As weeks stretched unexpectedly into months, Jim's absence saddened the boys and me. The weeks between visits seemed interminable. I found it difficult to discipline the boys. "Just wait till your father gets home!" seemed more idle threat than deterrent.

Jim's daily phone calls only made the separation harder. He reported that he was tired of eating in restaurants. His new coworkers felt sorry for him since he was alone and invited him for dinner. Often, he had invitations as many as four or five nights a week! His weekends were spent riding his bike, going to movies, exploring the new city.

I was pleased he had the opportunity to lead a seemingly carefree life, but soon I became resentful. I didn't have a carefree life. True, Jim spent long hours in the office, but once outside it, his time was totally his own. I, on the other hand, was completely responsible for the boys' homework and transportation. I, alone, cheered them on in sports, maintained all the finances, and kept an impeccable house in case of a showing. Plus the zillions of things that moms regularly oversee—laundry, orthodontist visits, and grocery shopping. Even with these added duties I felt guilty for resenting Jim's absence.

There was nothing he could do from so far away. He

missed going to the boys' games and being with us. He missed his home, and he missed his family. But I resented getting stuck with most of the work.

Our home had been on the market for five months. More than seventy-five real estate agents and clients had walked through without a single offer. The prospect that this living arrangement might continue even longer was frightening. I was tired. I was mostly tired of being so *responsible*.

One really rotten evening, my friend Bridgett called from Nashville to ask how I was doing. It is not only hard, but pointless, to lie to someone who has known you a long time.

When I said, "Fine" and my voice broke, she said, "Fine, huh? Anyone would know you aren't fine when your voice breaks on the little word *fine*."

She listened to me complain and cry. She heard my exhaustion, my aloneness. When I finished pouring out my self-pitying tale of woe, she quietly said, "Do you want me to come?"

I knew that Bridgett really would get on a plane to be with me. I was comforted. It wasn't that she had to come; it was that she *offered*. I knew she *heard* me. She didn't lecture me or accuse me of being self-centered. She didn't commiserate. She didn't try to talk me out of my point of view. She offered to come be with me.

Looking back on those six months of separation, I still shudder. I am so relieved that period of our lives is over. I often wondered then, and still do now, how single moms do this, day after day, without a break? Who relieves them? In my situation, I knew that Jim would return every few weeks, that our house would eventually sell, and that our family would be reunited. For a single mom, no one arrives every two or three weeks to alleviate her pressure. She makes all the decisions all of the time. She is *always* responsible—whether or not she acts responsibly. I admire the women who perform this job well.

I think of my friend, Bonnie Keen. A vibrant woman with sparkling eyes and breezy blond curls, she is a seasoned vocalist in Nashville's music industry. Bonnie is a *strong woman of faith* turned *woman of strong faith*. She is a full-time single mom. As she and I talked about both the peaks and ravines of her life as a single woman and parent, she peppered her conversation with easy but hard-earned laughter. Bonnie's path to single motherhood was filled with enough tears to "float a boat," but with the help of some devoted sisters, she is discovering new paths to joy.

Bonnie's Story

"Single motherhood was not something I ever imagined would happen to me," she said. "It was something experienced by others out there. To tell the truth, I didn't have much understanding or compassion for their decisions."

Bonnie, like many other Christians, assumed that any woman seeking divorce lacks stable faith. "I was brought up with a lot of works and righteousness. Then I found myself in a marriage I could not fix. I knew leaving was unavoidable. There was no way I could continue physically or spiritually. Even though the circumstances of the divorce were beyond my control, I felt tremendous guilt. That really was the beginning of God's teaching me about reliance upon His strength and not my own."

The most difficult resolution for Bonnie was the acceptance of God's grace for a new place in the social and parenting strata. This change formed a barrier in her mind that nearly broke her spirit. "Daily, the negative messages ran through my head: 'Your poor children will have to suffer. You can't be enough. You're not doing this right.'" The stress she endured through the divorce itself and then in the adjustment to single mothering finally forced her to a decision: "Either I was going to fall apart completely or I was going to have to find a new level of faith."

Part of that process for Bonnie has meant learning to honestly admit anger—toward God. "I can now shake my fist and cry. That's new." Before, she had no way of expressing negative feelings toward God. "There's a lot more to knowing the Lord than being afraid of Him. He is surely omnipotent, and we need to have a sense of awe, but I've learned to get into the boxing ring and fight it out a little bit. God is big enough for that. He is big enough for my disappointment, and for my doubts."

Those who have seen faith as a set of rules to be obeyed can understand Bonnie's frustration—*and* her relief. She learned that God is more powerful than her sense of shame. "I had not forgiven myself for my divorce. I had not forgiven myself for what seemed so wrong—being a single mother. Because my marriage failed, my sense of self failed."

When she landed at the bottom, she saw God's perspective. With the help of Scripture and godly friends, she began to see mercy and grace. "To deny forgiveness is, really, to deny Jesus and the power of what He did on the cross." Like well-trained bodyguards, mercy and grace led Bonnie safely away from the enemies of self-destruction and defeat.

Her advice to other women in her situation is "Forgive yourself, no matter what the circumstances." Bonnie mentions a particularly poignant moment in the Gospels when Jesus washed Judas's feet. If Christ didn't pass over His unrepentant betrayer, surely He won't pass over a repentant divorcée.

It is not easy to understand circumstances surrounding another's failures. Wise counsel should not be approached lightly. When Bonnie's pastor knew her story and knew her situation, he supported her. "In a way, he absolved me, if that's the word," she said. "He told me, 'You are so loved by God. Don't feel like a second-class citizen. See yourself as a daughter, not an orphan.'" Increasingly, as she rested in the cool wash of grace, Bonnie's hot anger toward herself and toward God was alleviated.

Bonnie found freedom in God's forgiveness that galvanized her emotional and spiritual health. It enabled her to forgive others as well. "The more forgiveness I walk into, the more I want to release for other people. If I am to be transformed by the pain I've gone through, and if anything good comes out of a divorce and single motherhood, it's that I have become more compassionate. I have, hopefully, come to be more bold with truth and filled with more grace than condemnation."

How have Bonnie's sisters made a difference in her journey? "God is merciful to single mothers," she affirmed. "He provides friendships to get me through. God has given me understanding and unconditional love from the women who walked with me in the crucible—women who were there to cry with me, pray with me, and hold on with me.

"Tori is my closest friend. She is one of those people who I can call in the worst moments and be absolutely honest with. She lets me be hopeless. She doesn't try to talk me out of it. She doesn't buy into it or encourage me to give up hope, but she listens and loves me through it."

Such amiability and calmness are vital, Bonnie said, because the emotions involved in divorce and single parenting are extreme and intense. Friends who neither panic nor assume your faith is substandard do the most good.

Tori guided Bonnie to treasure herself. Bonnie explains that this training is like the instructions given at the beginning of air travel: "In the event of an emergency, put the oxygen mask on yourself first, and then aid those around you." Tori often calls Bonnie to remind her to make room for some down time—to take a bubble bath surrounded by the candlelight or to enjoy something soothing and nondemanding. She occasionally kidnaps Bonnie for a day, and they escape to a locale where Tori does all the planning and cooking. "For a whole day, I can stay in my bathrobe," laughs Bonnie. Such love, the love of a friend, proves her estimation of her worth.

Carlana, another single mom, faithfully remembers Bonnie on days when the absence of a husband and father are most noticeable. On holidays that are gut-wrenching for a single person, like Valentine's Day, "Carlana will call me and break through those lonely times."

Another friend, Karen, occasionally writes notes that are "like a visitation every time, they're so powerful! I usually start crying because the message speaks so clearly from God's heart that I haven't been forgotten." Karen shares a scripture or just enlivens hope; she never judges or instructs. "It's liberating to be spoken to in that way," Bonnie affirms.

"One of the worst parts of single parenting is being in the

totally unnatural position of trying to be everything for my children. I just can't. And I can't always be perfectly composed. My kids have seen me in weak moments; they have seen me cry and they have seen my tiredness. We talk a lot and we pray together. I hope they also see a living, breathing, human person who cries but is also happy as a Christian rather than a one-dimensional, always strong Pollyanna."

Bonnie emphasized the importance of two things: first, the indispensable need for Christian women and men to care and help her with her children, and second, the freedom to let her kids be kids.

She cannot expect her children to parent her or to carry the load for the missing parent. "I don't take adult issues to my children," she said. "If I have a difficult decision to make, I call my family or Tori to talk it over. Single moms have to develop a network of adults for counsel."

Although many of Bonnie's friends have generously responded, there are still gaps. One is simply inclusion, granting the divorced woman a seat inside the social circle. "A lot of married women seem afraid to talk to you, afraid divorce will rub off or something," Bonnie said. Others act threatened by Bonnie's singleness. "Most women never expect to be divorced and a single parent. They don't quite know what to do. All of a sudden, you don't know where you fit socially. One of the most painful things for me was how I was suddenly left off of guest lists to social events I had been on for years."

Compounding her sense of rejection was finding that couples Bible studies meant just that. Where, with married men and women, was there room for the single mom? "I felt ostracized," Bonnie said. "I just want to be treated like everyone else."

Another aspect of the lone parenting struggle is not getting bogged down. "If I could encourage single moms—and I say this to myself—I'd advise not losing out on the miracle of what we're living in each day. What happened in the past must not be allowed to bog us down. My son is six and my daughter is eleven. They're going to be in this place only once in their lives. If I get tripped up in the difficulty (which is understandable), I will miss the miracle that's here. There's a way to deal with the hardship and still treasure the now."

Surviving single motherhood comes down to two simple directives, according to Bonnie. "First, go to the Lord. Rest on what the Word says, not what you feel or what society says." Second, take care of your emotional and spiritual health. "If your body is sick, you go to a doctor. Don't be afraid to ask for help. Pastors, friends, and counselors can help. Remember to put your oxygen mask on first."

The Story Goes On

When Bonnie speaks, her voice is bright and full of optimism. Her manner indicates how she has learned to meet each new crisis with hope in Christ. This quote from Ernest Hemingway moved her: "Life breaks us all sometimes in unexpected ways and some of us grow strong in the broken places."

This phrase motivated Bonnie to arrange a session with songwriter friends Darrell and Tori. Together they worked to express the hope that God will take tragedy and turn it to good.

Lay down your weary head
when the troubled waters flow
Life breaks us all sometimes
where we need to grow
Innocence is not a crime
in time we'll understand
And find the grace of mercy
sifting through the fingers of God's hand[4]

Bonnie is confident that we are given second chances for the future, under the comfort of mercy and grace.

The LORD is close to the brokenhearted and saves those who are crushed in spirit.   PSALM 34:18

3

Marriage:
When the Ideal Shatters

---

*"My failed marriage saddens me. I did
not choose this. I chose a home and
life where there was peace."*

Julia (not her real name) is beautiful. She is elegant, dignified, and gentle. Heads turn and conversations sputter when she approaches. She is a strong, determined career woman and the single mother of two sons. She walks with beauty and grace, yes. And she walks with God.

Her former husband is a successful evangelist. He is quite handsome and hands-down charming. But often, looks are deceiving. And often, so was he.

When Julia told me her story, I found it hard to believe. How could a successful and seemingly spiritual man treat his wife in the way she described? How could he so easily exchange a loving wife and two devoted sons for money, mistresses, and narcissism?

Appearances. When will we learn not to trust them as a basis for judgment? Do acclaim, success, magnetism, or popularity make us immune to deceit or sin? Because Julia's husband enjoyed fame, others advised her to stay with him. She was urged to endure his cruel and demeaning treatment. Her story of transition from married-with-everything to single-with-nothing illustrates that Christian sisters sometimes react by drawing near and sometimes by withdrawing completely.

Julia's Story

My children scampered through the door of my mother's house with hardly a backward glance. I hesitated on the front step, working to retain my composure. Clinging to my mother, I finally broke into tears. "This is only a temporary arrangement," I sobbed. "I'll come back for them as soon as I can." I broke from her embrace, ran to my car, and drove away. I did not see my children again for six months.

Leaving my mother's, I returned to my own home. I quickly shoved as much stuff as I could into my car and fled from thirteen years of familiar habits. For the final time, I left my husband.

Each of the three times I left before, I returned, believing his promise to change. Each time he begged me to stay, admitting he needed to be a better husband. His idea of better was to buy me a mink coat. Taking me to a distant island for romantic renewal, he swore undying love for me.

He *did* keep his promises—for a few days. But that which was so generously offered proved easily withdrawn.

I cannot say exactly when he began to change. At first, he became more self-absorbed. He demanded things be done his way, regardless of the inconvenience to those around him. He wanted more from everyone yet gave less of himself. He began spending ministry money carelessly, pleading for more from his audience. He scheduled first-class flights to ministry engagements; he insisted a limousine pick him up. He dined in elite restaurants and ordered expensive bottles of wine and champagne. He gathered an ever-present entourage to share his indulgences. Amazingly, he justified his behavior by saying he worked hard for the Lord: "I deserve a few rewards now and then."

Eventually, even I wasn't enough. The moral standards my husband preached no longer applied to him—at least that's what he said. I was baffled and devastated by his godless bevy of excuses. I was no longer attractive to him but younger women were. He called me his queen and referred to the other women as pawns, as if we were all players in a game. "They aren't taking away your position," he told me. "You have everything: a mansion, pool, and Jacuzzi, expensive cars, designer clothes, and jewels. You can buy anything you want." Then his new, cruel spirit threatened me: "Besides, you can't take care of yourself. I've had to do it all these years." His belittling intensified, and I believed him. I felt helpless. I wasn't pretty enough, smart enough, sexy enough. I felt I was being penalized for getting older and for having children.

On Sundays our fellow Christians were happy to see me in church, because I was a novelty and a local celebrity. I was an ornament, the lucky Mrs. I smiled; they smiled. But when I admitted my crisis, they didn't know what to do. They were afraid to help me. Part of who *they* were hinged on *our* success. For years we had made them look good, and now my husband's fame felt too good to forfeit.

When I cried out for help, the people of our church offered nothing but weary clichés: "Be patient; trust the Lord. God works in all things." No one, not one person, dared to stand with me. I was stunned. I was truly alone.

My husband's addictions to wealth, women, and luxury, plus his business failings brought great financial hardship. We lost our custom-built, six-thousand square-foot house. This was the home I had decorated and furnished, the home where our babies were born and where I expected to watch them grow up. But hoping my marriage would be redeemed, I left this home and followed my husband to the city he chose. It was, he said, "a great place for us to live."

I blindly followed with luggage and a few pieces of furniture, and we squeezed into a small, two-bedroom apartment in a downtown high-rise. My husband arranged our move and told me that the rest of our furnishings—which I loved and had painstakingly chosen—were being shipped and placed in storage. This was a new level of isolation. We lived in a new town in a cramped apartment with no place for the children to play. Sadly for the family, my husband found many places to play. He was rarely home, and a sense of abandonment was my constant companion. My children had no father; we had no friends, no money, no life.

There were times, standing on our apartment's balcony, when the Enemy whispered, "Go ahead, jump. Death is better than divorce. If you die, maybe your husband will change his ways, his ministry will be more effective, and many more will come to know the Lord." As I drove my car, my head filled with suggestions: "Go ahead, drive over the cliff. Death is a much better option than divorce."

Although I saw it coming, I feared divorce. For years I weighed the pros and cons of staying or leaving. Every day I looked at my children and knew they lived where the principles of the Lord and basic human decency were regularly compromised or betrayed. My soul withered in torment when I heard my husband lie again and again to our children. He lived by two standards: publicly it was "Praise the Lord!" and privately it was "Have a good time!"

The "what woulds" of divorce paralyzed me. What would my family think; what would my friends think; what would our followers think? Wearied by the lies yet terrified by the truth, I was afraid to stay and afraid to leave. My worries about losing my sanity were soon joined by concerns about my physical safety. My husband did not physically abuse our children, but his choices were damaging them emotionally and spiritually. For me, a new, gnawing fear persisted: *What if he gets AIDS? What if he gives me AIDS or some other sexually transmitted disease?*

In desperation, I phoned some women I knew who had chosen to stay with unfaithful husbands. "Tell me how you do it," I asked. These Christian women told me about the unrelenting cycles of drugs, alcohol, tranquilizers, and affairs. Their voices sounded hollow, dead. Their selves had been destroyed. I shuddered against that happening to me.

Panicked, I searched for a helping church. I looked for

Christian brothers and sisters who would walk with me, who could help me understand God's Word for this situation. God led me to a pastor and congregation that encouraged the unmuddling of my thoughts. They demonstrated their desire for my relief and helped me unravel the effect of lies. With their help, I discovered who does take care of me: God. My husband was not God.

Desperately, I prayed. I asked for clear direction, for wisdom, for strength, and for courage. I tried to transform the small, cramped apartment into a cozy home. Unpacking boxes and rearranging our few belongings helped to fill my lonely hours. One day I sorted through a stack of papers and found copies of the packing slips from the moving company. I was shocked when I read the receiving address for our furniture. It had not been shipped to storage but to the house of my husband's current girlfriend. His deception poured over the edge of my endurance. Lies, all lies. He had no intention of being faithful to me, to our children, or to our marriage. That day, I decided to leave.

That was the day I drove several hours to put the children in my mother's care, the day I crammed as much as I could into my car, the day I left the shattered pieces of my life behind. A friend insisted on going with me across the country toward yet another new town and another new start.

The pattern of sisters helping me began from the moment I decided to leave. As my friend drove, my thoughts wandered to the early days of my marriage. The man I loved led me to the Lord and nurtured me in the Word of God. We studied our Bibles and memorized scriptures together. He taught me to stand for what was right. We shared our faith and resources with people; he taught me to give. There was so much good—then.

I remembered that his influence greatly enhanced my life. I recalled the day he said, "My gifts are to teach and preach and minister on the stage. But what are yours?" I feebly attempted to think of something. He considered me a good conversationalist, so he encouraged me to join his office staff. I immersed myself in the work of the ministry, where I blossomed and grew, enjoying the opportunity to contribute my skills. During our early years together, we traveled extensively. I met and worked with a variety of wonderful, godly people: sponsors, sound and lighting companies, concession crews, managers, agents, and publishers. Supporters developed a ministry following, and I worked with them closely. Every day in those early, sincere years, my skills sharpened. My husband called me wonderful—then.

Now, driving through the deserts, mountains, and farmlands, I repeatedly asked God, "Am I doing the right thing?" The beauty of His creation calmed my soul. I felt His peace. Reaching my destination, I thanked God for my safe journey and asked His direction for the next step. I needed a job. Friends. A place to live. A church. Wisdom.

New friends came first. They lined up job interviews; they loaned me money to repair my car. Later, I realized that the moment I stepped away from the old pattern of life, I stepped into a new order of grace. I was eventually hired by a small company in a field completely new to me. I rented a duplex one mile from my office and began stabilizing the turmoil. After six months, plans for my children's school and care were finalized and we reunited.

The home we established would fit inside our former garage. I have learned what can be lived without. Like the apostle Paul, I can live contentedly without things, but I cannot live without God. I admit there are days I long for a top-of-the-line foreign car, but God has taught me the adequacy and fun of a small American car!

Daily, I am confident of God's working in my life. My neighbor, a single mother, has become a great friend. We baby-sit for each other, cry on each other's shoulder, and cheer each other on. She is beyond anything I thought to pray for. I never asked, "Lord, bless me with a neighbor who will be able to walk with me and I with her," yet He provided what He knew I needed.

I have inner peace; I no longer live another's lie. What people see in me is what I want to have seen—me, the real me. I thank God each time I see my children's happiness, every time I hear their laughter. They will be fine without luxuries. They cannot be fine without my integrity.

From the extreme of total submission as a wife, I have moved to the extreme of total responsibility for my own life—and my children's lives. All my decisions are made with them in mind. I look at life more seriously, and I cannot afford inappropriate associations, male or female. I consciously battle anything that counters my children's best interests. I've found that I, too, benefit from these constraints. We maintain a stable daily rhythm and schedule. Discipline reigns and a sense of order prevails. After too many years without it, we enjoy emotional security.

I was a little surprised when the Lord reminded me, after so much pain, that even though my husband abandoned his faithfulness, he contributed to my development. His encouragement to work in ministry had actually prepared me for this new phase of my life. The Lord made it clear that I was to thank my husband. Still emotionally afraid of this man, I decided to write a letter. And never mail it. The Lord continued to impress upon me that I was to thank him. Late one evening, I summoned the courage to call. My former husband was astonished by my voice and understandably amazed by my confession. I admitted that what I learned while working in his ministry built the confidence I now possessed. He appreciated my honesty and my thankfulness. After our conversation, I fell asleep, exhausted. I awoke the next morning free of the familiar and bitter sting. No longer chained to my past, I knew I could go on in my life.

My failed marriage saddens me. I did not want to be another divorce statistic. I did not choose this. I chose a home and a life where there is peace. And I chose honesty, obedience, and reliance on God's Word. I doubt, though, that I would have the compassion needed to help women enduring the same crisis. Now, I quickly tell them not to isolate themselves. Seclusion is dangerous, yet so easy in the face of shame. Doubt, too, isolates us. *Do people really believe us?* we wonder.

Reaching out and allowing people to help you requires making your needs known. If I were vulnerable and honest when asked how I was doing, others were able to minister to me. There *is* hope and healing for most divorced or separated women. But I have learned they must not sit and wait for it to come along. We must be willing to admit our need. It's amazing what happens to us in the company of truth and courage.

The Story Goes On

Fear of being judged by her fellow Christians kept Julia from leaving her unfaithful husband. Fear of being a single parent helped hold her in a loveless marriage. Confusion over God's will tormented her soul. Her story reminds me of the Israelites in Egypt working as slaves.

The entire Israelite community was afraid. They feared powerful Egyptians, plagues, and death. By following God's intervention through Moses, they finally left Egypt. Still they were afraid: now of crossing the Red Sea, of starving, of dying of thirst. They complained and longed for the old familiar misery!

Fear can cripple the best of us. Fear of the unknown keeps us tied to the familiar—even if it's harmful. Fear of the future freezes us in our present pain. Fear of what others think hinders us from the freedom of obeying the Lord. Fear of financial poverty ties us to miserable employment. Fear of being alone returns us, day by day, to destructive relationships. Fear of single-handedly raising children has caused more than one woman to risk abuse rather than seek a solution.

We need Moses as our guide. When he knew with certainty the call of God, he separated from the familiar. He listened to God's voice and, with help, learned to be resolute in obedience. Though the long journey from slavery to freedom was treacherous and complex, he remained steadfast. He knew God was with him.

As a sister to a woman like Julia, I need to leave my own

fears, my own preference for comfort. If I am to reach out, I must be willing to hear without judgment, listen without condemnation, and love without reservation. Jesus never compromised goodness, but He touched lepers, associated with sinners, ate with the despised of society, and loved to the death. He calls me to share His mission.

I will betroth you to me forever; I will betroth you in righteousness and justice, in love and compassion. I will betroth you in faithfulness, and you will acknowledge the LORD.

HOSEA 2:19–20

4

The Single Life:
Growing Strong, Growing Wise, and Growing Alone

———————

*"One truth prevailed. The Father does
not give His children bad gifts. His
joy enabled me to see my singleness
as a very good gift."*

I am married, and happily so. Occasionally, for fleeting moments, I wish I were single again. Usually, those thoughts surface on laundry days as I fold Jim's socks into pairs (seemingly hundreds!) or when I balance the checkbook and discover cash withdrawals he forgot to tell me about. However, every time I eat a deliciously seasoned home-cooked meal, I am grateful for my marital status. Jim is resident chef.

Some of my single girlfriends say, "You are so lucky to have a husband who cooks!" My silent reply is, "Yeah. You obviously don't clean up the kitchen after him!" But they do clean up kitchens—only the mess is their own.

I admire the self-confidence so many of my single sisters possess. They are singularly responsible for things I automatically share with my husband: managing car maintenance, filing tax returns, finding a place to live, and deciding just how to spend money—money they alone have earned.

Here is the story of a woman I admire. Her growth and her maturity and her honesty are examples to all women, married or single.

Cindy's Story

Like so many of us, Cindy dreamed. Now she laughs at herself, recalling her move to Nashville where she dreamed of becoming a star. She landed a job as a receptionist and never did taste stardom. Her move brought her much closer to life's hard reality of learning to rely on the Lord's sufficiency alone. Cindy's professional life has changed drastically, and she is currently Director of Publishing for a large Christian music company. What has not changed in her life is the Lord's sufficiency.

"I am an agenda-driven woman who sets goals and meets them," said Cindy. With her usual humor she continued: "When I was younger, I had it all figured out. I would be married by my mid-twenties, have babies, a successful career, the whole lot. But by the time my thirties rolled around with no real prospect of marriage, I began to feel that I was in some way defective."

The years passed, relationships of short duration came and went, and Cindy waited, wondering just how long she would have to wait for the gift of marriage. Other areas of life seemed well in hand. She had a satisfying job, strong friendships, and a stable relationship with God. Her love and obedience to Him and her years in Christian ministry unintentionally gave way to an unspoken expectation: God would bring her heart's desire—a husband, family.

Then, in her mid-thirties, she met "the one." It couldn't have seemed more perfect. John (not his real name) was her age, a Christian, fun-loving with a great sense of humor. He was a virgin and a medical student with a financially secure future. Could it be more perfect? Yes. It could have been, but it *seemed* right. Cindy gave her heart away.

"What more could I have wanted? I was so ready for a man of his caliber that I mistakenly ignored warning flags. It took me two and one-half years to realize that the relationship was not right. Meanwhile, much of my relational energy was used trying to convince John that he was capable of making a commitment to me, to us. At the same time, I worked to convince myself that I could love a man I would have to talk into marrying me.

"The hardest thing I've ever done was to admit the relationship wasn't the gift I thought it was." Breaking up with John meant putting off the fulfillment of her dream. "Suddenly, I feared that my most fruitful years were passing. One of the most significant hopes of my life had again eluded me. For the first time, my singleness was a reality I had difficulty accepting. With John gone, I felt great loneliness. I yearned for love, deep, significant love. I could not imagine going through the rest of my life without marriage and motherhood, as these were my heart's desires. Why, I wondered, *why* would my Savior withhold such good things from me? Had my heavenly Father handed me a stone?" (Matt. 7:9)

It is not hard to understand Cindy's questions. When our hopes and expectations of God are dashed, we often come dangerously close to feeling like God has given freshly baked bread to others and has handed us a cold, hard stone. That is exactly what this vibrant, humor-filled woman felt.

"Cynicism began to tinge my personal and spiritual journey. My perspective grew narrow and angry. I measured God's goodness to me, His love and His power by what He had and had not given me so far. It is hard to admit, but it all added up to profound and deep disappointment."

The result was that Cindy's love for the Lord shifted to obligatory obedience. "I believed, I even obeyed, but I would no longer risk my heart. I felt unrelenting grief over the lost hope of marriage. It hung over me as I approached my thirty-ninth birthday, that sobering day that would remind me that the big 4–0 was just around the corner. Depression hit hard." Only, instead of going to bed and pulling covers over her head, Cindy got busy strategizing "a frantic search for places where I might meet godly men." Between social activities and long hours at work, she binged on shopping excursions. Anything "to keep God and sorrow at bay."

"My efforts exhausted me. Both inside and out, I grew weary of my intense disillusionment with God. Anger, resentment, and irritation haunted my heart until one day over lunch a friend shared how some revival services were drastically changing lives of people at her church. She, too, was changed. I wasn't interested. I couldn't get into the idea that God would use anything that I wasn't capable of controlling. It sounded like dependent emotionalism to me. In my usual sew-things-up fashion, I had long ago decided against quick-fix Christianity. I would stick with the traditional approach and not set myself up for future disappointment with God.

"I listened politely to my friend, but the only effect her story had on me was to heighten my desperation. *She* had tasted of God's joy in a new way, and she had found peace. My friend said that for the first time in her life, she no longer lived out of her past. She was free from her lifelong fears. I snapped angrily, 'I *don't* want to hear any more! You're talking about a God who's given you something very special. He isn't doing that for me, and I can't stand to hear about one more thing I can't experience!'

"My pain churned inside me for several days. I muttered and mumbled to God about my sorrow. Then one morning I awoke with an overwhelming sense of grief; I ached with spiritual disillusionment. Without either planning it or controlling it, I began to pour out my confessions. I told Him everything—my resentment over losing a chance at love, my sense of God's betrayal at keeping me from my heart's desires, my unabated anger. Then I admitted my greatest fear: that even if I invited God to meet me in my disappointment, He might not show up. That would be more than I could handle."

But God did show up. "Suddenly, my heart began to break. But instead of brokenness, there was a profound sense of wholeness and unexplainable joy. Missing were the cynicism, resentment, and emptiness that had for so long filled my heart.

"I laughed, I cried, I didn't know what was happening. I was no longer in control. My grief turned into a wild, fierce joy. I was overwhelmed by a flood of tremendous emotions.

My thoughts and prayers turned to thanksgiving. One truth prevailed. The Father does not give His children bad gifts (Matt. 7:11). His joy enabled me to see my singleness as a very good gift."

Everything changed for Cindy. Her time with God was now motivated more by desire than by obligation or the clock. Her expression and works of faith emerged from love rather than duty. As she began enjoying the Lord, her desire for a husband's love diminished. "I can truthfully say now that I have tasted of His joy, and it deeply satisfies. Psalm 94:19 is a personal testimony: 'When anxiety was great within me, your consolation brought joy to my soul.'"

Cindy was amazed by the patience of God as her loving Father. She remembered a confession by Oswald Chambers that rings true of her own heart. "Lord, I have had my misgivings about You. I have not believed in Your abilities, but only my own. And I have not believed in Your almighty power apart from my finite understanding of it."[5]

No longer, says this single woman of God. "Now," she says, "I confess the truth of Psalm 73:25: 'Whom have I in heaven but you? And earth has nothing I desire besides you.'"

The Story Goes On

Everyone dreams. Everyone faces choices. Women hold many of each in common: dreams of happiness, security, love, and success. Daily choices of what to wear, what to say, what to eat, what to sell, what to buy. Lifetime choices of how to relate, whether to work, how to handle aging, how to raise children. The choices of marriage, faith—the list refuses to come to an end. Married women and single women also know dreams and choices unique to their status. The distraction of dreams and choices must not prevent the building of sisterhood.

Cindy knows that the foundation of her contentment is Jesus Christ. Sisters in the Lord can take the materials of prayer, conversation, activities, counsel, and confessions to build striking structures of friendship—from the foundation up.

Listen to advice and accept instruction, that you may gain wisdom for the future. The human mind may devise many plans, but it is the purpose of the LORD that will be established.

PROVERBS 19:20–21 NRSV

5

Successful Women:
Where Do They Go?

"Where do successful women go? Where do harried, overscheduled women go for rest or counsel? Where do strong women go to be weak?"

A characteristically strong woman may possess an innate capacity to endure flurries of sorrow or crisis. She buckles down or digs in to survive life's storms. But when the winds blow in gale force and the rains threaten to drown her, where does she run for cover?

If you are usually the strong one offering a helping hand, who, when you need help, comes to *your* rescue? How easy is it to admit your ebbing energy and growing weakness? Can customary self-sufficiency and strength actually become weaknesses?

Lori (not her real name) finally staggered out for help, drenched and losing her way in a storm of uncertainty. I tried to help steer her to safety. Amanda (not her real name) was literally paralyzed both emotionally and physically. Tina (not her real name) picked her up and carried her, figuratively and literally. Here are two stories of women nearly decimated by the power of another's fury. Each weathered the turbulence under the shelter of a sister.

Lori's Story

My friend Lori easily balances the duties of wife, mother, teacher, and Girls' Club director. Her bubbly, outgoing personality qualifies her for the title Mrs. Congeniality. She knows no strangers and her quirky, outrageous humor is contagious. Keeping a schedule bound to fatigue the strongest, Lori works inexhaustibly yet always has time to offer an encouraging word. She is extremely sensitive to the needs of "her" people: her children, students, church family, and friends. In Lori's presence, everyone feels comfortable and valued.

Lori's husband, Keith (not his real name), is different. His relationships with other men seem shallow. He is distanced and detached. Outwardly, he appears satisfied, assured, and self-sufficient. But as Lori eventually discovered, inwardly he was despondent and depressed. To assuage his secret misery, he sought solace in other women—many other women. Many of them were Lori's friends.

Gradual changes appeared in Lori as she absorbed her husband's deceit. Signs of stress surfaced: a sharp word, too quick an answer, impatience with her children. A strained, tight-lipped smile replaced her trademark grin and familiar laugh. When asked how she was doing, a subtle but visible tension betrayed her confident "I'm fine."

Lori could not talk to anyone in her church about her husband. She did not want to betray him or air their dirty laundry in public. She feared the misunderstandings or the repercussions that might occur. She rightly feared the harsh judgment of her family—Keith is the pastor of their church.

So an outgoing but suffering young woman longs for help. Sadly, Lori's unmet needs to talk confidentially and honestly with someone are all too common. Strapped by difficult situations, women in visible leadership roles or wives of prominent men often hesitate to seek a listener. Dangers impede the process of getting help when seekers fear appearing unsuccessful or fear being condemned.

Where do "successful" women go? Who comforts the evangelist's wife? The spouse of the chairman of the board? The famous musician's wife? The local elder's wife? The woman behind the successful businessman? Where do harried, overscheduled women go for rest or counsel? Where do women in the public eye who juggle the tasks of children, career, church, and relationships find refuge? Where do strong women go to be weak?

Highly visible women in the shadow of a husband's career, especially wives of men whose success has a spiritual dimension, face untold and countless stresses. Tireless critics monitor their every move. Their attitudes, countenance, children, and even housekeeping abilities are watched and judged.

Our expectations of public women soar. Many of us expect from them the toothy smile of Miss America, the gentle servanthood of Mother Teresa, the cooking finesse of Julia

Child, the decorating abilities of Martha Stewart, the parenting techniques of Dr. Dobson, and perhaps, the spirituality of the Pope.

We, her observers, expect her to wear appropriate clothing of just the right shade, length, fabric, and fit. Her accessories must not be gaudy or too expensive. Her properly dressed, freshly scrubbed, and well-behaved children should exhibit the mental capabilities of young Einstein or, at the least, display the politeness of Miss Manners. If asked, her watchful public would gladly assign her a life verse! "I try to please everybody in every way" (1 Cor. 10:33).

Usually, though, when a woman tries to please everyone, she actually pleases no one. What happens when she cannot live up to internal and external expectations that, in truth, are unhealthy and unrealistic? Women who muster the courage to admit their needs are often rewarded with appallingly shallow responses. "Well, just pray about it." Or "Give it time; it will all work out for the best." Too frequently they find that issues not quickly resolved are criticized and rebuked. "Do we have to talk about this again?"

Please hear me carefully. Prayer and time are God-given resources through which He directs us. We are specifically instructed to pray about everything. This is not because prayer is like medicine: take two sessions; wait four hours for relief. Rather, prayer is conversation—with God. He knows we talk to those we trust, those we allow to influence us. From the example of Jesus, we learn to privately express our innermost thoughts to God. However, God also has designed for us community. We, His people, are commanded to give and receive aid, love, counsel, and comfort. Believers are called to be His physical representatives; a compassionate, human hand to hold and a strong arm around us during times of personal crisis not only help comfort but are essential to our healing.

Following a recent telephone conversation with Lori, I felt frustrated by her hesitant, guarded answers, by her resistance to my inquiries concerning her. I remembered the apostle Paul's reference to Phoebe. He asked Roman Christians to receive her "in a way worthy of the saints." Then he instructed them to "give her any help she may need from you, for she has been a great help to many people, including me" (Rom. 16:1–2).

Phoebe, like Lori, was a highly visible woman. She was a deacon, and it seems she was also a wealthy patron and hospitable hostess. At the least, her work and faith were great enough to cause recognition from Paul, who spoke of his indebtedness to her. But Phoebe was in need. Of what? We are not told. Maybe she needed assistance in her business, perhaps accommodation, rest, or encouragement. Whatever it was, Paul placed the responsibility of aid on her community, on her fellow believers.

After rereading the two verses in Romans concerning Phoebe, I committed myself in a new way to Lori. She had once seen me through some difficult personal times, and now it was my turn to encourage her.

My first job was to accept that I was responsible for my attitudes and actions toward her; I was not responsible for her response to me. I assured her of my love and reminded her I was committed to our friendship, no matter what she faced. I telephoned her frequently, and often we met to talk at a park while our children played. We met as friends. We both knew I did not fully understand her pain; it was enough that I chose to stand by her in it.

Lori told me, "Some days it's just not worth it. It's so hard to keep going, not knowing how it will all end." Wounds of betrayal, isolation, and helplessness became too much for her to bear. Though she believed Keith's aloofness was an attempt to camouflage feelings of worthlessness and incompetence, she felt incapable of helping him. I had no perfect answers, but I could provide love and a shoulder to cry on.

Lori gathered the courage to seek professional help and legal counsel. She was relieved to find compassion and wise direction. Her subsequent actions spurred her husband to seek counsel as well. He resigned from the pastorate, and now they are both in the process of healing. Even in their instability, they hold on to their faith. In the midst of Keith's confusion and Lori's uncertainty, they know their ultimate healing comes from the Lord.

Amanda's Story

When an accident paralyzed Amanda, Bob (not his real name) speculated that it was "God's way of telling her to be more submissive" to him. Bob's relationship to his wife darkened. Unreasonably, he refused to carry Amanda down the apartment's two flights of stairs—even for doctors' appointments. He forbade Tina, Amanda's best friend and faithful visitor, to take her to church services or to movies. He expected Amanda to sit on the couch all day in her pajamas. Amanda had no idea then that behind Bob's controlling domination and insensitivity was his sexual infidelity. His frequent absences, his flagrant passes at Tina, and finally his diagnosis of herpes spurred Amanda to decision.

Amanda did not want divorce. Tina did not advocate divorce. But Amanda knew that she could not continue as she was. She was husbandless except for his control, housebound and deteriorating. When she was led to read Ezekiel 16:6–7, she knew it was time for action: "Then I passed by and saw you kicking about in your blood, and as you lay there in your blood I said to you, 'Live!' I made you grow like a plant of the field. You grew up and developed and became the most beautiful of jewels." Amanda wanted to live. She wanted to develop into a beautiful jewel. And this meant asking her abusive husband to leave.

Now paralyzed and in great pain, how could she begin this transformation? She still needed someone to carry her physically, spiritually, and emotionally. Enter a sister's care. Under the circumstances, Tina's dedication to Amanda was nothing short of astounding.

Every morning, Tina drove to Amanda's apartment and made breakfast before attending morning classes at a university. She returned to prepare Amanda's lunch, then took the train into the city for her internship. After work, she went back to Amanda's to prepare dinner before her evening classes. At the end of a wearying day, she drove home.

"She became my legs," Amanda said. "She saw obstacles and overcame them. If I complained I couldn't get the wheelchair up a small step, Tina would quietly say, 'I can.' She was like Simon of Cyrene who carried the cross of Christ. When I couldn't carry my own cross, she carried it. Every day, her arrival was a reminder of God. She did more than talk to me, she became what God is. She washed and oiled my feet. She did not preach the Word of God; she was the Word of God." Tina personified the thought of Saint Francis, who said, "Whenever possible, preach the gospel. If necessary, use words."

Tina wrote notes of encouragement to Amanda helping her to realize her potential as a person regardless of her physical limitations. Tina also urged Amanda to continue singing, privately and publicly. "I challenged her to go on because there were people who needed to hear what she had to say. It had to be from her, from the place she was, from her in *that* condition."

"When I couldn't attend church, Tina brought the church to me on a cassette," Amanda said. "She also brought books for me to read during the day." A single paragraph in Philip Yancey's book *Disappointment with God* fueled the change in Amanda's life. She read the account of Peggie Woodson's twenty-three-year struggle with cystic fibrosis. Peggie's minister quoted from William Barclay: "Endurance is not just the ability to bear a hard thing, but to turn it into glory." Peggie noted that her minister "must have had a hard week," because after he read it he banged the pulpit, turned his back to the congregation and cried.[6]

Amanda and Tina identified with Peggie and the minister's response to Barclay's words. They were exhausted, but wanted to endure for future glory.

Amanda's physical dependence on Tina lessened with the purchase of her own car and with her move into an apartment with wheelchair access. Her self-esteem and self-sufficiency increased when she began volunteer work with troubled youth. Even with the satisfaction, though, came trepidation and fear. "I loved the work and the youth. But now with my handicap I was afraid—afraid of how I could cope physically and how the residents might respond to me. I soon realized that fear is a handicap many women encounter."

With Tina's encouragement, Amanda started giving concerts and telling the story of her dependency on God's faithfulness. "You can't let circumstances control your faith," Amanda told her listeners. "Make sure your faith controls your circumstances. In the same way, my wheelchair doesn't control me; I control it. I direct the wheelchair where to turn, where to go, where to stop."

Their Stories Go On

Lori's and Amanda's stories remind me of the resurrection of Lazarus. When Jesus arrived at His friend's tomb, He ordered the mourners to remove the sealing stone. Martha, Lazarus's sister, tried to intervene, imagining the horrific smell from the deteriorating body. The prospect of bad odor and decay apparently did not deflect Christ's compassion and loving miracle. At his friend's command, "the dead man came out, his hands and feet wrapped with strips of linen, and a cloth around his face." Lazarus was newly alive, *but he was still draped in death* (John 11:1–44).

Several thoughts occur to me. First, why didn't Jesus blast away the rock with a single word? Instead He asked bystanders to remove it. Then, surely, the miracle of Lazarus could have included new, clean clothes. Instead, remnants of death dangled from his resurrected body. Why?

Jesus required family and friends to unwrap Lazarus so they could *participate* in his healing. Imagine the joy and the laughter mixed with tears as they gathered around Lazarus to unravel the cloth strips from his body and to untie the knots that bound his hands and feet. The same people who wrapped his lifeless body for burial now joyously unwrapped him, freeing him to renewed life.

Any pain, our own or that of a friend, can be odorous and impossible to ignore. In grief or crisis, human hands are often the tools for removing the bandages that cripple our minds and our souls. Sisters are not professionals. Few of us are masters of psychology or theology. Sisters are friends, faithful friends, who dare to touch wounds. Sisters are women who dare to stand near decomposing situations and women who risk that their association implies approval or complicity.

I loaned strength to Lori; Tina offered limitless support to Amanda. Invisible wounds slowly respond to a gentle, healing touch, a merciful ear, or a kind word delivered by a counselor, friend, or a sister. Whether you are the giver or the recipient, Jesus stands nearby, pleased with the process.

But when they were oppressed they cried out to you. From heaven you heard them, and in your great compassion you gave them deliverers, who rescued them from the hand of their enemies.   NEHEMIAH 9:27

6

Children:
When Beauty Comes
Wrapped with Struggle

*"You want to throw blame somewhere,
and it is a lot easier if you
blame yourself."*

    Deborah Craig-Claar is artistic and theatrical, passionate and expressive. Our friendship blossomed when we worked in the same office for a few years before I married Jim and before she left to pursue graduate degrees in theater and education.

Now, many years later, we meet at least once a year at events in the gospel music industry. We try to schedule a few minutes together to catch up on our careers, husbands, children, projects, and lives.

On one occasion, I was chattering on about Elliott and

Taylor, bragging about their accomplishments and commenting on how well they were developing for their ages. I showed Deborah pictures of them, then asked if she had any pictures of her children. Smiling, she pulled a photograph from her wallet and handed it to me. Her daughter Jessica was seated, holding her brother in her lap. It was obvious from the first glance that something was wrong with Benjamin.

I was embarrassed. I had strutted my children out like trophies and flaunted their superiority in physical appearance and size. I felt trapped by my own words. Now what was I supposed to say?

I'm not sure if my discomfort was evident, but Deborah seemed more subdued than earlier in our conversation. As she got up to leave, I wondered if my remarks had hurt her. Deborah could be very private with her emotions, especially negative ones. Suddenly I knew I could not let our time together end this way. She was a friend I did not want to lose over something I said or did not say.

She paused in the doorway. "By the way, have I ever told you about Benjamin's handicap?"

In that moment, I realized she was as worried about my feelings as I was about hers. I smiled, wrapped my arms around her, and said, "No. But please tell me now."

We returned to the table and talked for almost an hour. I confessed my confusion and asked her, "What do I do? Do I ask about Ben? Do I tell you about my boys? Should I acknowledge Ben's handicap? Do I ignore it?"

Her answers led me into a new level of understanding. I have asked her to tell her story so you, too, will know better how to help a sister with a handicapped child.

Deborah's Story

Deborah's first pregnancy with Jessica was unusual only in her significant weight gain of sixty pounds. When Deborah and her husband David decided to try for another child, she took off the extra pounds from her first pregnancy and, to help insure her health, took prenatal vitamins for two months before conceiving. She carefully cut out caffeine and other potentially harmful substances; she didn't even take aspirin. But as soon as she knew she was pregnant, she sensed something was wrong. Oddly enough, weight was her clue.

"At four months, there was almost no external sign that I was pregnant," Deborah said. "My doctor assured me I was, and we always heard a heartbeat. But it seemed like forever before I felt the baby move, and when he finally did move (I felt it was a boy), the movements were abrupt and jerky instead of the fluid rolling and pushing I felt with Jessica. In my journal I wrote, 'I keep thinking he's hurting. When he moves, it seems like he's in pain.'"

Deborah, a practical and strong woman, distracted herself by finishing the coursework for her doctorate. But the differences between pregnancies were too noticeable to dismiss. Remarks from others that would have cheered her during her first pregnancy—"You're pregnant? You don't look it!"—did nothing to assuage her apprehension. She was never completely comfortable with her baby's progress, but she faced her fears privately. Deborah had few relationships in which to unburden herself since her four closest women friends lived in other cities. She and David were between churches and walked a solitary road during this worrisome period. In addition, her fear of looking foolish contributed to my friend's discomfort.

"I wasn't sure there was a problem, and there is a part of you that thinks about how stupid you are going to feel when you tell people there's something wrong and there isn't," Deborah admitted. "I would liken it to calling the police when you are worried about a sound outside your house. When they arrive and it's nothing, you feel dumb."

Following a sonogram at six months, her doctor changed the baby's due date from May 23 to June 7, saying casually, "Oh, it's probably a smaller baby, but not off the scale." Deborah thought, *What scale?*

The situation got scarier. Over the next two months, her doctor changed the due date three more times. When the baby's head size prompted a full-term date in August, her doctor recommended that Deborah see a specialist. This doctor took X rays that measured the baby's bone growth rather than just the baby's head. He determined that the baby was thirteen inches long and weighed only two pounds. Alarmed, Deborah's doctor immediately sent her to a hospital with an elaborate intensive care nursery for an emergency cesarean section. The day was May 5, just three weeks from her original due date. As staff prepped her for the birth, Deborah's new physician explained the diagnosis.

The baby was a victim of interuterine growth retardation, which resulted from an incorrectly formed placenta. There was nearly no amniotic fluid in the womb, nor had there ever been, which explained the baby's jerky movements. The baby hadn't been nourished properly, which explained his weight. Consequently, the baby might have some serious defects, which range in this disorder from deformity to mental retardation.

The doctor quickly assured Deborah that there was no known cause for this condition. Even if it had been discovered earlier in the pregnancy, nothing could have stopped or changed it. The baby had only a 50 percent chance of surviving the birth, but if he did, his two-pound birth weight gave him about an 85 percent chance of living. "The baby's in great distress," the doctor stated solemnly, "and has been for a long time. But the fact that he's alive shows he's a fighter. That's a good sign."

Deborah was brokenhearted yet strangely relieved to have her fears confirmed. In those brief moments before surgery, "I prepared myself for my baby to die," Deborah said. "I also prepared myself for my baby to live with any number of handicaps."

Ironically, after all the months of worry, the one emotion she felt least while awaiting surgery was fear. "I wasn't scared. I was just waiting to see what would happen. In the face of such an enormous range of possibilities, I couldn't pray for any particular outcome. For once, my own desires weren't in the way of God's. He knew what was best and knew what would happen. I did recognize one fear for myself if the baby had profound handicaps: How would I cope? How would I face the challenge?"

Statistically, some babies born with interuterine growth retardation eventually catch up to healthy babies in both size and mental capacity, but there was no way of predicting how Deborah's baby would do. Deborah remembers that the delivery room was filled with hospital personnel and machinery. It lacked the relaxed, cheerful atmosphere that surrounded her daughter's birth. "Everyone was poised and focused. No one tried to force small talk, and I appreciated that."

The delivery itself happened quickly. Deborah heard a frail cry. It was a boy, as she predicted. "He was so incredibly tiny," she noticed. His head was somewhat bigger than the rest of his body, but not strikingly so. "I remember David saying he looked fine." The couple named their son Benjamin.

As Deborah looked at her infant, she noticed "his eyes looked scared. I remember saying two things to him. 'Hello,' and then, 'I'm sorry.' At that instant, I felt overwhelming responsibility that I had done this to him. I was overcome by an awesome sense of failure."

Benjamin stayed in the intensive care nursery for five weeks. It was almost immediately clear that he would live. Specialists offered no grim predictions for Benjamin. Deborah said, "They told me, 'We could tell you the statistics for other babies born with this condition in the last ten years, but those stats say nothing about *your* baby.' They put no limits on what Benjamin could accomplish, and that was extremely helpful."

Deborah left the hospital after four days, but returned daily to visit her son and provide breast milk, which doctors recommended for its antibodies. Deborah's milk had to be fortified with extra nutrients, though, for Benjamin's growth. "It was just one more thing that made me feel inadequate," Deborah said.

Finally, at four pounds two ounces and sixteen inches long, Ben went home. Deborah missed the hospital's support and understanding. "Something kicks in while you're in that environment," she said. "You find an extra source of strength. And at the hospital you realize that for the baby's sake, you have to look at the positives. That was easy to do since so many babies around him were in much worse shape than he. But when I was alone, I was scared and felt weak."

Life at home was an adjustment, even though there was nothing special Deborah had to do for Benjamin. "He was not on a monitor, and I had no tests to perform, but he still seemed completely helpless. Even so, I thought that having survived so far, he would be fine. I never had the classic middle-of-the-night panic to see if he was breathing like I did with my daughter. I knew Ben was a survivor."

As the second child, Ben missed out on the welcome a first baby excites. The uncertainty of the situation—Ben's condition, concerns about his health, fear of saying the wrong thing—kept visitors away. Deborah didn't take it personally. "I'm sure people didn't know whether to say 'Congratulations' or 'I'm sorry.'"

Shannon, Deborah's good friend, bridged the awkwardness by remarking, "He looks real healthy, don't you think? He's just real small. How small is he?"

Her forthrightness and upbeat spirit were "astonishingly refreshing. That was *exactly* how he looked. Shannon offered me no hand-holding, sympathy, fears. Instead she offered just curiosity and chatter." She responded to Ben in the same way she had to Jessica.

Other responses were downright humorous. Deborah took Ben to the grocery store in June, while he still weighed only four pounds. The woman ahead of her in the checkout line looked at Ben, gasped, and said, "Do you know how small your baby is?" At the time Deborah just said "Yes," but wishes she'd quipped, "I know. I gave him a bath this morning and he shrank."

Other innocently spoken comments weren't so easy to ignore. One woman Deborah encountered at the post office asked if Ben "would make it." A security guard at the college where she taught assumed Deborah must have caused his tiny stature by "walking too fast." Strangers' stares and comments constantly reminded her that Benjamin was different.

This type of comment prompted Deborah's original fear that she somehow caused his handicaps to return with gale force. Over and over, she reflected on her pregnancy. "You scrutinize every day," she explained. "I had the flu at three months, and I didn't take any medication. I tried to get a doctor to say that affected the pregnancy. There was nothing unusual that I did physically, except I didn't slow down. I took grueling comprehensive exams when I was six months along: three days straight spent writing exams. I was concerned about my pregnancy but went ahead with my schooling.

"I felt I had been very selfish. I had not put the baby's interests first. I convinced myself that I shouldn't have gotten my Ph.D., at least not then. I should have waited."

Though doctors assured her that Ben's condition was completely unrelated to her activities, completely unpreventable, Deborah still needed a scapegoat. "You want to throw blame somewhere, and it's a lot easier if you blame yourself," she said. "I would look at him and catch a glimpse of the boy he should have been. I still feel it's my body's fault, even though I had no control over it. After being convinced that I had no physical means to blame, I turned to my own sin.

"I thought I was being punished, that God was taking

out His wrath on me," Deborah continued. "I was upset because I felt He was taking it out on the wrong person, on an innocent little baby. I went through a time where I tallied every sin I had ever committed and assumed Ben's handicaps were the ultimate payback."

While coping with these feelings, Deborah felt the additional strain of talking with other mothers. "For the first three years of Ben's life I had real difficulty talking with women who had normal children his age. When I listened to their complaints about preschool and toilet training, I was thinking, *you don't know what problems are.*

"At the ages of two and three Ben was still speaking single words. He didn't walk until he was past two. Mentally, he was at least six months younger. The biggest frustration was communication; we had no idea what he was saying because it just sounded like gibberish. And it was impossible to know how to discipline him. Time out wouldn't connect in his mind. I had no idea how to either model or shape his behavior.

"Bad days were when I saw only what he couldn't do instead of what he could do. I avoided going to places where he would be with children his own age. That only highlighted his differences."

One conversation demonstrates her frustration. Deborah chatted with a church friend. They talked about Ben for a few minutes, then about the woman's children, who were accomplished and skillful. When the friend boasted that her daughter had made honor roll for the fifth time and her son was learning a new instrument in band, Deborah fell silent. "I didn't want to talk about Benjamin anymore. I didn't want to talk about any kids.

"The hardest thing about being with parents of normal children is when they compare. Reality is okay, but not comparisons. 'He holds that crayon very well,' not 'He can't draw with a pencil yet, can he?' It's good to talk about Benjamin and where he is, what he's learning now. But if a woman says, 'Golly, he's eight years old and he can't write his name yet!' or 'Shouldn't he be speaking in sentences by now? My two-year-old does,' that's painful. Mothers of handicapped children are keenly aware of the differences between their children and others. We don't need it pointed out."

Describing Benjamin's condition is a special concern. For the mother of a mentally challenged child, many words hurt. Deborah said, "Benjamin is retarded, and that is the term we use to describe him to people who ask what's wrong with him. But *retard* is one of those words people have used callously for too long. It's demeaning."

Understandably, Deborah longed to talk to other women in similar circumstances, but no support groups existed for parents of children with Ben's condition. Then, when Ben was three, Deborah began to find relief in the company of women who faced similar challenges. Benjamin joined a special preschool where all the children had some sort of learning disability. "All of the kids had things they couldn't do, but they all had things they could do too," Deborah observed. "I saw their mothers every day. These women had special stories about their children, and they spoke freely about their fears."

Here at last was a place where Deborah could talk and be understood, and where her son had a place to shine. She began to see Ben's personality rather than just what he could or could not do. "I finally relaxed and realized Benjamin would always be on his own schedule," she said. "I stopped keeping track of every little skill he could and couldn't handle. My child cannot be molded like a lump of clay. He was created by God; all I'm doing is guiding him and feeding him physically, emotionally, spiritually. Ben is who God made him to be. To try to disassemble the work of the great Designer means to destroy Ben's person and potential."

The Story Goes On

In retrospect, Deborah needed more sisters to lean on during her fearful pregnancy and especially during the early days of Ben's life. A steady listener might have helped her sort and smooth her fears. A wise sister might have spoken grace to her when she thought that God made a dart for each sin she'd ever committed and then sent them spinning toward her son.

Deborah has learned hard lessons and from them advises sisters to be sensitive to one another. Sisters should seek out the mother of a handicapped child, especially if they know her experience. Ask about her child, and celebrate the child's successes with her. Allow such mothers the freedom to withdraw from a conversation that is suddenly painful to her; keep talking, but relieve her discomfort by introducing a new subject.

There is much to celebrate in Ben's life. Today at the age of eight, he is a curious mixture of "cans" and "can'ts." An energetic, happy child, he's enrolled in a special education second grade. He can write his numbers to 100, but still can't tell you his phone number. He knows his alphabet, but not the difference between today and tomorrow. Deborah says Benjamin is a daily source of surprise and joy. "He's a constant reminder that we're all a combination of abilities and disabilities. We have no standard to meet but God's."

Isn't the freedom to be who we are as God's children, to develop at our pace, the desire of us all? My relationship with Deborah has become a more honest exchange. Now I feel the freedom to tell her about my children, and she keeps me up to date on the progress and development of her own. We have learned that our love for each other is cemented by our mutual interest in each other's lives, which includes our children. Every year when we meet, we bring pictures of our children to show each other. I think the two of us show a picture of progress and development too. We're all doing very well and have much to celebrate.

Even though my illness was a trial to you, you did not treat me with contempt or scorn. Instead, you welcomed me as if I were an angel of God, as if I were Christ Jesus himself.

GALATIANS 4:14

7

Parenting:
When Love Brings Pain to Your Home

---

*"I realize that children truly are a gift
for a season. There's no guarantee
how long we will have them."*

After fifteen years of marriage, our dear friends Bud and Kristy decided to adopt a child. For nearly twelve months they waited for a phone call from the private adoption attorney. Bud continued his work as an accountant, and Kristy continued her work as an executive assistant. Then, on a hectic Friday morning, the call came.

"Can you take a baby boy home today?"

"Today?"

"Yes, today."

"We're not ready. We don't have anything. We have no crib, no clothes, no baby stuff."

"I'll call you in the morning for your answer."

"Tomorrow?"

Overnight, Bud and Kristy's lives changed. When Saturday's dawn closed the long prayerful night, they both knew: *This is our child. We must go get him.* They felt the Lord had given them this child, a son.

By Saturday noon, they were active parents; buying diapers, borrowing a crib, learning to sterilize bottles, scheduling for the baby and themselves.

Learning of this instant parenthood, their church welcomed the new family Sunday morning. Friends gathered around them, admiring the baby and congratulating the parents. Laughing, the pastor announced the child's middle name, Richard. "You'll just have to wait to hear his first name," he told the congregation, "until Bud and Kristy choose one!"

That same evening the church hosted a surprise shower for the new family. They received every imaginable thing: stroller, high chair, car seat, blankets, toys, and enough baby paraphernalia to fill several nurseries.

By noon Monday, Bud and Kristy were childless. Over the weekend, the birth mother changed her mind and demanded back her child.

The news stunned them. They felt so clearly, so strongly, that the Lord stirred the feeling that this was their child. Were they wrong? They loved the child at first sight, and then he was torn away from them. Why?

As friends, we were at a loss for what to say. What was

appropriate? How do you express sorrow without sounding trite, without mouthing dry platitudes?

I called Barry, a business acquaintance of mine, that week. He and his wife had experienced this same type of loss with a foster child years earlier. This subject was not freely discussed, especially by his wife Sarah. Because I ached so for Bud and Kristy and needed advice from someone who could give me appropriate understanding, I called anyway.

"Would your wife," I asked Barry, "be willing to talk with me? I don't know what to say to Kristy. Maybe Sarah can tell me what to say."

"I'll ask her," Barry answered, slowly. "But I don't know if she can talk about it yet."

Surprisingly, Sarah agreed to talk with me. The next morning, over hot biscuits and steaming coffee, she talked. And talked. And I listened.

Sarah's Story

Barry and I were college students and married by age nineteen. We worked hard, were successful and contented with our lifestyles. We were so contented that we wanted no children. Barry had a vasectomy at age twenty-five. But as we neared thirty, we realized success just wasn't enough.

We talked about children, a family. I had never been around small children, didn't baby-sit for friends, and wasn't sure if children were the something that was missing. A friend asked if I had ever considered taking in foster children. "No!" I quickly replied. "I think it would be too hard to give them up."

A few weeks after that conversation, I received a phone call from social services. My name had been given to them by a mutual friend, and a child needed a place for just two weeks. The child was slated for a third foster family, but the woman there was ill and needed time to recuperate. "Would you consider helping us out? It's just for two weeks." Silently, I wondered if this would help me to determine if a child was the fulfillment I sought.

I called friends to borrow a crib, diapers, and other baby stuff. That very day I went to pick up the baby. I saw a six-month-old girl propped in the middle of the floor, dressed in a dirty T-shirt and smelly diaper. *I cannot take this child*, I thought to myself and left the room.

The child began to whimper. "Why is she crying?" I asked.

"She's afraid you're going to leave her," was the reply.

It wasn't love at first sight, as I recall. I just took her because I felt pity for her. The child's birthmother was a child herself, a thirteen-year-old runaway incapable of caring for a baby.

My transition into motherhood was not smooth. I did not know how to care for an infant, especially one who cried so much. I felt guilty because I wasn't patient. I thought I was supposed to love her at first sight and have a natural instinct for mothering. I didn't. I struggled to break through the baby's resistance to being cuddled and held. It was as if she believed I would desert her, just as she had been deserted by her own mother and two previous foster mothers. She tensed when I lifted her. Even at her young age, she seemed to mistrust women, including me.

Still, I tried to take good care of her. The two weeks

stretched to four and included a period of hospitalization for the child. Barry and I stayed with her around the clock, which surprised a staff nurse. "Many parents drop off their own children and walk away. She is just a foster child and yet you stay."

For me, the child was primarily a responsibility and almost a burden. The child's natural family had let her down. I just wanted her to be treated right. But for Barry, parenting was instant joy; he was a natural father. Watching him play happily with the child pierced my heart, making me feel even more guilty for my lack of attachment.

The weeks stretched to months. The baby passed through all the expected infant progressions: teething, crawling, climbing, walking, and talking. Little by little, I began to enjoy her. As the child blossomed, so did I. Our time together grew easier, more relaxed. There was more trust, more laughter, and, I realized, more love.

During these months, the third foster family rescinded their offer to take the child into their home. Around the same time, the natural mother's sporadic visits convinced me that she could not possibly care for her own child. I began to resent the mother's visiting rights.

It was harder and harder to let social services pick up the child and take her to the mother's house. I didn't want her to see the baby. She didn't even know what her daughter liked to eat. She knew nothing about her own child. I dressed her like a doll for these visits only to have her returned wearing a dirty diaper or clothes I had never seen before. To say I was upset is an understatement.

As Christmas approached, Barry and I warmed to the idea of a child in our home for the holidays. A transformation occurs at Christmas when you have a child! Everything was for her: the tree, the decorations, and all the gifts. I had never had a Christmas as wonderful as the one with her!

We took her with us to a Christmas party. Our friends commented, "This cannot be the same child we met a few months ago! When we saw her the first time, she looked so lost. Now she looks so loved."

Loved she was. I looked forward to each day spent with this little girl who now called me Mommy. We played, kissed, tickled, and giggled; our hearts entwined.

Celebrating her first birthday, Grandma and Grandpa came for their "first grandchild's" party. We were a family.

We took lots of pictures. As a child, Barry's mother lived with a foster family, but never carried their name. Her natural father refused to allow her adoption. She never had pictures of herself as a baby and suffered from a lack of personal history, of truly belonging. So with great deliberateness, we tried to capture this child's infancy. *Someday,* we thought, *she can look back and know that as a baby she was healthy, happy, and loved.*

Eleven months passed. We had an active, healthy eighteen-month-old toddler on our hands—and we loved it. In one more month, reported social services, the natural grandparents would lose their adoptive right, and adoption plans could proceed.

Two weeks before that year ended, the natural grandparents announced their interest in adopting this child they had rarely seen. I was stunned. For nearly a year she had been in our home. We had taken care of her, fed her, sheltered her, and loved her. And now she might be taken away.

Panicked, Barry and I pleaded with a judge to assign a

guardian ad litem to the child to insure she would not be placed in an unhealthy situation. We lived through two weeks of agony waiting for the judge's ruling. We loved her and wanted the best for her, and, to us, the best meant she stayed with us.

With each passing day, our hope grew. On the eleventh day, the doorbell rang. When I opened the front door, my heart froze. A social services officer was there to retrieve "my" little girl. "We have the legal rights to this child," the representative stated coldly. "We have the right to put her in your home, and we have the right to take her out."

"Don't take her away from us!" I screamed. "She's ours. We went to the judge because we felt you are not doing what is in her best interest. She has a chance for a normal life here!"

But they did take her away. We waited through four torturous days before we stood, once again, before the judge. When he ruled in our favor, our hearts leapt with joy. He questioned the suitability of the natural mother's home and demanded that a thorough study be completed.

"Except," interjected social services, "the child has already been returned to her mother."

Angrily, the judge shouted that she was not to be moved again. "The child has been moved too many times. Though it is not fair to this couple, I will not move her again!" To the social services representatives the judge menacingly added, "I will investigate what is going on in your offices."

It was over. Nothing could be done. We left the court empty-handed and empty-hearted. Social services met us at our home to collect the child's belongings. They packed most of her clothes. They gathered up some of the toys. I handed them the photo album with all the pictures. The empty crib and her framed first-birthday picture remained in the room. And her smell. And the echo of her laughter.

Dominique. Her name was Dominique.

For three months I lived numbly. Barry and I tried shaking our misery by taking a trip. It didn't help. I could not stand to be in the house alone, so I went back to work. Some days, I found myself driving through her neighborhood, hoping to catch a glimpse of her playing outside. At night, I could not sleep. When I did drift off, a child's cry wakened me. Then I heard only silence.

I could not even cry. I was too angry. In my fury, I even phoned social services to shout, "You do not care about children or the people who do care for them. You only care about your system!"

And I was angry at God. We begged and pleaded with the Lord to let us keep Dominique, but we lost her. I just couldn't believe that the Lord had this planned for all of us.

Friends meant to offer solace when they said, "The Lord will take care of you. He will give you another child." I didn't want another child. I wanted *her.* I did not need assurances that God knew best. I needed understanding. I needed gentle treatment for a badly bruised heart and spirit.

I wish someone would have listened to my feelings, even if I sounded unbalanced. I didn't want to be told things would be okay. I wanted to talk but no one wanted to listen. Everyone wanted to tell me it was going to be all right or that they knew how I felt. I wanted to shout, "No, you don't know how I feel! You don't know how empty, frustrating, or helpless this feels!" Sometimes I just needed to be held. If someone had held me and let me cry, it might have made it a little better.

Somehow, though I was spiritually spiraling downward, I clutched hold of some kind of faith. It *seemed* God was not there, but I knew He was. In my weak faith and strong anger, I tried to hold on. Healing, I later learned, was a process.

In the midst of our grieving, Barry flew to St. Louis where a specialist reversed his vasectomy. I began seeing a therapist, mainly because I could not bring myself to clean the nursery. I could not pack up the little dresses. I could not remove Dominique's clothes or gather the toys into boxes.

Often we didn't think we would make it through, but eventually Barry and I began to release our anger, cry in each other's arms, and talk about how much we missed her. We held on to the hope that what happened to her would turn to good.

Fourteen months later, I was pregnant. I was thrilled, but my excitement was overshadowed by my emotional pain. When Sean was born, I didn't want him to take Dominique's place. It was wonderful to hold my son, but along with that sweet baby's arrival, my nightmares began. Again and again I relived the day they took her away. I was afraid I would lose Sean. On his first birthday, I was deeply depressed; I remembered her first birthday and my grief overtook me.

When Justin was born one year later, I knew that the time had come for me to give Dominique's things away. I was finally ready and needed to let go of her.

I try to understand the purpose in all of it, I admit. I accept it, but I don't understand it. I can only trust that God used me as an instrument in her life, knowing I could handle it and she needed it. Maybe it was important for her to have both a mother and a father at that time in her life; we loved her and she knew it. We have to trust the Lord was, and is, taking care of her.

Today, I love my boys. I treasure my time with them, maybe more than I would have had it not been for her. True, we argue and yell and live in a normal home, but I work hard for my sons to have wonderful memories of growing up. Their childhood is precious to me. Because of our experience with Dominique, I am actually aware that children truly are a gift for a season. There's no guarantee how long we will have them. How we live with them while we have them is what matters.

The Story Goes On

I came away from my time with Sarah emotionally drained. My thoughts turned to how I take my own two sons for granted. *Would I do things differently with them,* I wondered, *if I thought they would soon be gone?*

When I arrived home, there was a message on the machine to call Bud and Kristy. When I heard Kristy's voice answering the phone, I knew something had happened.

"He's back!" she fairly shouted. "He's back for good."

"Who's back?" I asked.

"Our son." Kristy paused. "Jeffrey Richard. His name is Jeffrey Richard."

This time I knew what to say. "Treasure him," I said. "He is a gift for a season."

8

Friendship:
A Big Partnership through Small Tasks

"For the first time, I saw Jesus with skin on."

Whatever possessed us to buy a puppy? I suppose it was partially the sentiment that all boys need a dog to love. And, in all honesty, it was a way to put an end to our sons' begging. Adding a cocker spaniel to our household was like having a third baby, only worse. You can diaper a baby. A puppy's appearance in our family leads me to the story of Trace.

Trace's Story

When the Balins revealed their plans to adopt a child after ten years of marriage, they were advised "get a dog first and see how that goes." Actually, an abundance of advice was offered. Some of their friends were overly encouraging: "It doesn't matter how they arrive as long as you end up with at least seven. Start filling your quiver with as many little ones as you can!"

Others were not quite so enthusiastic. "Why do you want to lose your freedom? Kids will ruin your life!" "How do you know what an adopted child has encountered before coming to you?" "Doesn't it bother you that you won't be *real* parents?"

One friend of Trace's summed up motherhood this way: "It's joyous, it's depressing; it's exhilarating, it's drudgery; it's wonderful, it's awful; but nothing this side of heaven compares to a mother's love for a child."

Trace longed to know that kind of love: a mother for her child. Parenting was an experience she did not want to miss. A physical condition stole her opportunity for pregnancy, and adoption was the avenue to the promise in Psalm 113:9: "He settles the barren woman in her home as a happy mother of children."

The way to building their home filled with children was unknown and long. It began in a meeting with fifty other couples at the county adoption service. "After our background was checked," said Trace, "we were told our chances for getting a child were minimal. On paper, we did not appear suitable or stable. I am seven years older than Joel, and we are professional musicians. A young birthmother was likely to choose a financially established couple with the wife at home rather than the complicated home of a singer and a guitarist."

They were told they might have to wait up to three years

for a child. By then, Trace would be forty years old and past the age limitation.

Disappointed but determined, they inquired at another agency about the availability of an African-American baby. They were rejected; Trace and Joel are white. They asked about a racially mixed child. They did not qualify; the child would have an identity crisis. Trace and Joel were told children lose ancestry, history, culture, and tradition living with any race other than their own.

Trace wrote on the bottom of the application form that they would take any baby, any race, any sex. Responding to the comment, the agency referred them to yet another adoptive service that specialized in international adoption.

Finally, hope appeared. Korean baby boys could be adopted by couples in the United States. *How ironic,* thought Trace. *Biracial children are considered incapable of, or harmed by, identifying with white parents—but Korean children aren't.*

The pace of hope picked up unexpectedly when after three months the Balins were notified that they would, very soon, receive a baby. A week later, Trace and Joel stood nervously at an Atlanta airport gate waiting for the plane bringing adoptive infants, including their six-month-old son. "The babies deplaned last," Trace remembered. "Everyone who got off the plane stayed to see the baby passengers handed to the waiting parents. Applause filled the terminal as they placed Robbie in my arms. I tell people he was delivered from the belly of an airplane!"

Filled with hope, Trace still wondered if she could love as her own a child she did not carry and deliver. "My doubt was instantly erased as I took Robbie in my arms and looked into his eyes," Trace said, smiling. "My tears of joy cemented

our family as I held this incredible blessing from God."
Appropriately enough, their Robbie arrived on Valentine's
Day.

Instant parenthood presented the same adjustments faced
by all families with the arrival of a baby. During the first six
months, Trace and Joel couldn't remember ever sleeping for
more than forty-five consecutive minutes. Still, they fell into
the love and rhythm of parenting and soon thereafter felt
again a strong nudge of God. Watching a television program
hosted by their adoption agency, they saw pictures of homeless children flash across the screen. Seeing the sad little face
of a Korean girl, "There was a quickening in my heart," said
Trace. "I heard the Lord say, 'She is your daughter.'" Trace
raced to the phone to call the agency to claim the little girl
as her own.

"We hoped you would see her," they told her. "Two
previous adoptions of her have fallen through. Legality and
policy kept us from calling you, but we felt you were a perfect
match. Because," they added happily, "she is musically gifted
and wants to be a missionary when she grows up."

Three months later, on Thanksgiving Day, nine-year-old
Cecilia was their daughter. If Robbie's arrival was a major adjustment, Cecilia's proved an even greater challenge.

For starters, Trace and Joel underestimated the difficulties
of a language barrier. Cecilia spoke absolutely no English and
arrived with a rebellious attitude resulting from the rejection
she experienced in Korea. Her own parents gave her to an
abusive family, who in turn sent her away to the United
States. Cece, as she was nicknamed, thought she was going
to a country where everyone was rich and arrived with noth-

ing but the clothes on her back. The very opposite was true: the Balins had second-mortgaged their house to pay for the adoptions. Robbie was also making an adjustment. Though just a toddler, he was old enough to protest a rival, and he hated her on sight.

Complicating the blending of these four family members was persistent illness. Trace's lingering chest cold turned into a case of pneumonia that demanded a hospital stay. Two weeks after Trace left the hospital, her doctors discovered cancer in a case of endometriosis. They scheduled a complete and immediate hysterectomy. Concurrently, the Balins joined a church where they knew no one. Trace felt the pressures mount.

"In the space of just ten months, I was the mother of two children—an infant and a nine-year-old who spoke only Korean," she sighed. "All they knew was this sick woman. Cece was trying to adjust to a new country and new family; Robbie was trying to adjust to a new sister, and Joel and I were trying to adjust to them. I once cried in the shower for twenty minutes, wondering if I had ruined all our lives."

Trace's surgery put her flat on her back for six weeks. This was anguish for the professor's daughter who had been raised to believe she could do anything. Trace had flourished in an atmosphere that encouraged self-reliance. "I was never taught to rely on others," she said. "It was always fed in to me that I could be resourceful, that I had intelligence, and that there were no barriers for me."

The now constant burden of an achingly slow and sore body, combined with the needs of two children and diminished income, forced Trace to reconsider her autonomous pride. "I had always considered myself a real facilitator. God had to humble me."

A song Trace would later record had its roots in reality:

> *Life is hard and pain is real*
> *But the strongest hearts are not made of steel*
> *They're made of tenderness and trust*
> *Sometimes life has its way with us*
> *And we find it's the heartaches, struggles, and scars*
> *That make the strongest hearts.*[7]

Adding to the stress was the fact that the young Balins didn't look a thing like their parents, causing stares and unsolicited remarks. Trace remembers a woman commenting that Robbie was really cute, but "I just don't know how you could bond with a child that you didn't give birth to, particularly one who doesn't even look like you."

Trace swiftly replied, "God adopted us, and even though we're fashioned after his image, we probably don't look exactly like him, either."

She leaned on Ephesians 2:19–20: "You are no longer foreigners and aliens, but fellow citizens with God's people and members of God's household, built on the foundation of the apostles and prophets, with Christ Jesus himself as the chief cornerstone."

Despite discovering and sharing insights like these, Trace and Joel's faith wasn't a stronghold at that point. They had been Christians for five years, but they were still assimilating into the family of God. "We were still growing in the Lord," Trace explains. "And exploring. This was the first time we had plugged in to a church."

Both she and Joel had been raised with a humanistic view that cast a cynical shadow on everything they saw. "For us to go into a church filled with strangers and say, 'Yes! We're all family, and isn't this a wonderful thing?' did not ever appeal to us," she said. Consequently they were passive participants in their spiritual community, what Trace called "armchair Christians."

Nevertheless, one day when Trace was resting on the couch, feeling splintered before God, a knock came at the door. Trace opened the door to face a group of women from her new church. "We're here to help."

Their help extended beyond good wishes. Trace marvelled, "For *six weeks* they cleaned our house, did the laundry, provided all the meals, watched the kids, and oversaw our daily lives, saying 'Don't worry, lie back, we'll take care of it.'"

The result was complete transformation for Trace. "For the first time, I saw Jesus with skin on. When strangers are willing to give of their time and their energy and their resources in order to meet your needs, it changes your perspective of Christianity as a whole. It's one thing when you study it on paper, read it in the Word. It's another to see it acted out. Christianity was no longer just theology.

"I saw that it's okay to have needs," Trace says. "And it gave me a desire to serve others. I saw the power of the small task. Most people feel like they have to be some great athlete, some great singer, some articulate speaker. They feel they have to have a personality that creates importance. But I saw the relevance of the small task and the power that it can have in changing people's lives. Even in the simple act of someone feeding you, you're also being fed spiritually because you're seeing the Word acted out simply."

Trace later joined a home Bible study group and, for the sake of easing Cece's transition into American life, began homeschooling. Trace would not have known about these possibilities, or attempted them, had she not been involved in the community of the church. She and Joel embraced praise and worship music, which led them from cynicism and doubt to a joyous expression of faith and belief. They moved from questioning to seeking ways to serve. Trace began giving back the kind of help she had received, cooking, cleaning, and baby-sitting for other women who were in need.

By joining the community of women in her church, Trace found emotional and spiritual wealth. Here was a safe place to healthily vent the joys and frustrations of motherhood, a place to admit that it isn't always a pretty sight. Sisters encouraged her to expand the use of her vocal gifts and facilitated her growing ministry by tending Cece and Robbie when she was away performing concerts. Today, the Balin family is healthy, thriving, and spiritually lively.

At a time of desperate need and loneliness, Trace discovered the special strength of women in kinship. "I left behind this independent, self-minded human being, a woman actually more worldly than spiritual," Trace said. "I wish more women could experience the kind of friendship that takes place within the body of the church. It's not a private club; it's open to the public. If anyone would like to come in, they would be readily embraced." She urges women to search for that welcome because of its effect on her family's stability and well-being. "If women knew the kind of love and bond that there is in sisterhood, they'd race to embrace it in a heartbeat. And it creates a legacy, a chain that's unbreakable.

"I have certainly changed as a result of motherhood," said

Trace. "In fact, my family's biggest difficulties these days are not with our children, but with our pets! Our dog growls at us and gnaws on things like Robbie's leg. Our guinea pig lies like a rug in his cage all day until the prospect of food jump starts him to action. Our socially maladjusted cat has chewed a big hole in our mattress, christened the living room rug, and clawed her way to the top of our dining room drapes.

"Pets are not the pride of our parenting skills, I am happy to say; our children are. My recommendation is that if you want to get a pet, try adopting children first!"

The Story Goes On

Trace adopted Robbie and Cece and brought them into her own home to love, nurture, and provide for them. The women of the church adopted Trace. They cared for her at home when she was recuperating from surgery. They committed themselves to communicate with Cece and assuage Robbie's animosity.

A *group* of women arrived on Trace's doorstep to tackle the task of the home. Sometimes help is best offered by individuals, it is true. But in this case, "many hands made lighter the load." It takes only a few hours for a group to change beds, empty the dishwasher, vacuum the floors, read stories to children, and prepare the meals. I'm sure there was a lot of laughter and a healthy sense of accomplishment mixed with the hard work. There is no question but that both the providers and the recipients benefited from the work.

How easy is it to recognize a woman in need of assistance? Is it easier to help a close friend or a well-known member of the church, than to offer help to a newcomer or an outsider?

How often are we "Jesus with skin on"? As importantly, how often are we reluctant to admit we need some help? When we insist we are quite self-sufficient, thank you, we deny others the opportunity to practice healing arts. If life teaches us anything, is it not that we all need practice? Let us give one another the chance.

Trace wished "more women could experience the kind of friendship that takes place" in the church, where "they would be readily embraced." Do you encourage this level of friendship in your church? Trace believes that "if women knew the kind of love and bond that there is in sisterhood, they'd race to embrace it in a heartbeat." Is this evident in the place where you worship?

Think of the places where women of the church can make a difference to other women: in homeless shelters, in abuse centers, in crisis pregnancy homes, in after school childcare. How can you be "Jesus with skin on" in your community? Your actions, like those of the women who befriended Trace, do set an example to the women around you: your sisters, your daughters. There is only good news in the truth that the relevance of the small task can change a woman, a family, a church.

In love he predestined us to be adopted as his sons through Jesus Christ, in accordance with his pleasure and will—to the praise of his glorious grace. **EPHESIANS 1:4–6**

9

Abuse:
A Woman's Scar,
A Child's Wound

*"God's greatest treasures are often shown
against a backdrop of black."*

    I heard the muffled thud. My stomach instantly knotted, adrenaline flooded my system. Before I even heard the scream, I shot from the garage into the front yard like a runner out of the blocks.

    Rounding the corner of the house, I saw my three-year-old holding a golf club. My one-year-old was holding a golf ball. He had run to pick up the little ball without noticing his brother's powerful swing. There was nothing I could do. My baby was so stunned by the blow he could not inhale. Blood gushed down from a forehead wound, and his T-shirt became instantly blood-soaked.

The angled slash was small but deep. No permanent damage had been done, but as the emergency room physician finished a fourth stitch, he explained that the internal gash needed much longer to heal than did the surface skin. My son would have a headache for a few hours, he said. "And," he quipped, "he will have a small scar to remind him to stay away from golf balls."

Now, years later, a slight scar shows on my precious son's otherwise flawless skin, and I think of what scarring implies. First, where there is a scar, there is a story of injury. Whether by accident or intention, a wound occurred and rarely does a wound occur without pain. For some, like my son, both pain and healing happen quickly, and the scar fades. For others, the pain endures for decades, the scarring is sensitive, and much of it is permanent. Wounds of childhood are often evident in adulthood.

Caroline's (not her real name) Story

Why is it that brilliant things are often set against a backdrop of black? Diamonds on velvet, stars against a moonless night, a single raindrop on a mushroom's dark curved edge. Likewise, the value of life frequently glows against dark backgrounds. I am amazed by God's ability to illuminate our worth against dark sorrow. As I mulled over that thought, I realized that probably all of us have in our lives, somewhere, something very black.

With great clarity, I recall grievous episodes of my childhood. Not until I was an adult did I realize that my early years were not normal. With the exception of my grandmother, my childhood did not leave happy memories.

My childhood home was kept dark. No matter the hour, lighted cigarettes in the lips and hands of my parents glowed. My mother was a concert pianist. My father, a frustrated genius, was stuck in a menial job because there was no other work available. Both were alcoholics. Their drinking began every morning and was sustained well into the night. Both parents walked around the house naked, and my parents were openly sexual with one another.

My twin sister, Elizabeth (not her real name), was as introverted as I was extroverted. I was most obviously the parental favorite among four siblings. We have two brothers: one older, one younger. Accordingly, I received the most attention and affection from our mother and father. As much as my father favored me, he seemed to loathe my sister. In retrospect, she suffered his neglect and was spared his violence.

My life was forever altered when my father's affection turned inappropriately toward me. At first, he fondled me. Then, before I could name my confusion, he raped me while my mother watched. She did not try to stop him; she did not rescue me. When he finished, she seared my memory with her loathing. "You are just a slut, and you never will be any good." I was a child, not ever again childish. Never again did I trust my mother or father.

When my sister and I were about eight years old, our family moved to another state. In this new place, my parents' drinking escalated. We children called our maternal grandparents from a nearby shopping center and asked them to come for us. We had lived there for three weeks with little food to eat, and my baby brother was so hungry he ate laxatives from the medicine cabinet. When my grandfather arrived for us, the police arrived at the same time and took my father away. It was nearly thirty years before I saw him again.

My mother took her four children back to my maternal grandparent's house, where, for nearly a year, we lived in the basement. My mother hated her mother but would not drink in front of her. Her solution was to substitute over-the-counter medications for her alcohol. Compulsive spending became another high. Later, the damage from the years of alcoholism resulted in paranoia and mental illness.

On the one side, I knew nothing good. On the other, my grandmother was introducing spiritual things to us, and she took us to church. Around noon on a Good Friday she called me into the kitchen. "When Jesus was on the cross, Caroline," she told me, "this is what He did for us. The soldiers offered him vinegar to drink." Pouring vinegar into a glass, she handed it to me and said, "I want you to taste this. I want you to know what Jesus experienced two thousand years ago when He died for you and for me."

There were powerful women in my grandmother's family. She came from a line that believed women were important, that they were just as important as men. Our family had good minds, she often told us, and we had a responsibility to use them in the presence of God. God had given us these gifts, and God had a plan for our lives. The women in my family were well educated, especially in contrast to women of their day, and they were rightly proud of it.

My grandmother was a teacher, and she used every opportunity to teach us about God. One spring, ivy had grown into the garage, and my grandmother sat me down in front of it. "This ivy has grown without the sun," she pointed out. "See how weak it is, how it lacks color? This is what a life is like without Jesus."

I didn't fully understand it then, but I never forgot that illustration. She encouraged all of us to be the best persons we could be. In the midst of our family craziness, I got the message that I could conquer situations and develop my capabilities. By my grandmother's example, I was impelled to improve my life.

Despite her condition, my mother moved with the four of us to a house of our own. Except during school hours, we children basically reared ourselves. When I try to understand what happened next, if I try to make sense of human wounds, I can only do so by believing that God is able to bring beauty through scars.

I was about twelve when my older brother influenced several of his friends to lure me into a cave. What was first presented as fun got completely out of control, and I was gang raped by my brother's friends. My tears and pleas met impervious disregard. They finished and left me there. In my aloneness, a part of me died. My shame was too great. My grandmother's call to rise above circumstances failed in such a dark situation. Shocked and in complete denial, I got up, dusted myself off, and said to myself, *This never happened to me.*

High school was an academic escape from the agony of my daily life. I constantly struggled with the meaning of life and was not at all interested in boys or typical teenaged activities. *Life,* I told myself, *will begin as soon as I leave this town.* After graduation, and after a year at secretarial school with my sister, Elizabeth married her high school boyfriend. At age eighteen, I moved myself to Washington, D.C., where my career began as a clerk typist in the Navy department. On lunch breaks I went alone to art galleries.

My Avon lady shared my love of art and music and took an interest in me. While I smelled perfumes and sampled cosmetics, she asked questions. It was not long before we were friends. Nor was it long before she invited me to consider joining the National Symphony Auxiliary. I had no idea the purpose of the auxiliary was to raise funds for the symphony. In my usual focused style, however, I raised more money than anyone simply by making phone calls.

You don't always live remembering the reasons you feel the way you do. But now as I reflect on this occasion, I do vividly remember the effect of the past and its darkness on events in later life, regardless of how light they may be. Because of my involvement with the symphony auxiliary, I was invited to the White House for a tea by the first lady, Jacqueline Kennedy. I did not go. I did not go because I was ashamed. Ashamed of being alive.

Guilt is tied to events; shame is tied to essence. I was never without the feelings of shame. I thought something was wrong with me. Boys were often interested in me in high school, but I was never interested in them. In Washington, for the first time I fell in love, but I thought he wasn't that crazy about me. During this time, my mother visited me during a respite from a mental hospital stay. Her obsession with my life was intolerable. In an effort to escape her, to escape the memories of my father that surfaced in her presence, and to avoid my feelings for my boyfriend, I moved to California.

My first apartment on the west coast was situated just above the apartment of a single Jewish law student. In the evenings I sat on my balcony, he sat on his, and we discussed Christianity. I told him how he could become a Christian, but when he asked, "Aren't you a Christian?" I replied, "No, I'm not."

"How do you know you're not a Christian? You seem to know everything. You must be a Christian."

"No, it's not personal to me," was my answer.

God was important to me, my grandmother saw to that, but I knew I did not belong to Him. He was not real and not personal.

I remember that the week before my father moved us out of state, an aunt had taken my sister and me to church. She marched us to the pastor and announced that we did not know Jesus as our Savior. "I think they should receive Him before they move," she stated.

The pastor led us in a prayer to receive Christ. It wasn't real, at least not for me. I felt as though everyone in the church was watching me. I was humiliated and nothing else. The Christianity I saw here was not winsome, yet it held importance for me later because of my grandmother's faith.

When my new Jewish friend challenged me, I easily surmised that I was not a Christian. Mark 4:25 says: "Whoever has will be given more; whoever does not have, even what he has will be taken from him." This is exactly what I experienced on that balcony. I had nothing because it wasn't personal, and it was all taken away from me. I threw away any belief I carried from childhood.

Much to my surprise, my boyfriend followed me to California, got a job, and soon we married. In the years that followed, another aspect of blackness entered my life—emptiness. My husband was handsome, he had a good job, we had one beautiful child, and we owned a lovely home. Materially, I had everything I could desire. Yet when friends asked "How are you today?" I answered with "It's a bad day at Black Rock."

This was an intuitive phrase. Everything I thought I needed for happiness—a man who loved me, a family, a nice home, a meaningful place in the community—felt empty. I spent the days watching old movies on television. When my son began school, I was terrified that he would be molested. I connected that fear not to my own childhood but to a sense that I lacked control. My inability to control pushed me to the edge, and I began to plot my suicide. I felt guilty for not being content, and I felt powerless to protect my child. Nothing made sense, so I thought *why don't I just end it?* Remembrance checked me. My grandmother had instilled in me that I was not helpless, so I thought *okay, there's something I'm supposed to do.*

In an attempt to put meaning in my life, I started a college course in existentialism. Since high school I had read voraciously and agreed with existential writers who claimed that life is basically meaningless. I agreed that the only important question in life is "Should we or should we not commit suicide?"

A twenty-four-year-old married mother, I was trying to convince classmates to embrace existentialism. In the very first class session, after I expressed my beliefs, another woman my age began to speak. I knew clearly by her gentle tone that she was a Christian. In the weeks that followed, Linda (not her real name) pursued me as a friend and shattered all my images of what being Christian meant. She often called to ask how I was doing. She saw something in me, something glowing in the darkness, even when I gave speeches against the miracles of Jesus and remained adamantly agnostic. She didn't try to convert me; she tried to be my friend. She bought a gift for me when my second child was born. Such gestures of kindness were totally unfamiliar to my experience.

Our friendship developed, and Linda brought her children to my home to play with my children. Walking through my home, going from one room to another, she sang. *What does she have to sing about?* I wondered. She was happy. I was unsettled by this.

Linda and her husband had to go away for a weekend, and I offered to keep her children. When she said she would pick them up on Sunday morning in time for church, I offered to bring the children there. I fully intended to attend the service and even convinced my husband to go with me. Because of Linda, I was beginning to think that I should read the Bible. I was drawn to her faith.

On Sunday, sitting in the pew next to my husband, I listened to the pastor announce the text for the sermon. Everyone took their Bible and flipped through the pages. My face was red; I did not even have a Bible, let alone know how to "flip" its pages. I felt awkward. Someone pushed a Bible my way, and I fumbled for the book of Matthew, feeling completely humiliated. My husband said, "Look in the index," but I wouldn't do that. So I turned to where it looked like other people were. I was ashamed. I thought I was so smart, but here I was lost.

The pastor read: "Honor your father and mother." *I ought to be able to do that, but I hate my parents,* was my reaction. It was not humanly possible to honor them. Sitting in the surrounding pews, people looked happy. I wanted that, but

I didn't know how to get it. If it meant I had to honor my parents, it wasn't accessible to me.

When Linda called me later in the afternoon, I admitted I wanted to become a Christian. I wanted a life like hers; I wanted to sing; I wanted my life to have meaning. But if it meant I had to honor my parents, I was stuck. Linda was my first true friend and demonstrated it by answering, "Of course, you hate them. Who wouldn't? They were terrible to you."

Then what was I to do? "If I can't honor my father and mother," I asked her, "how can I become a Christian?"

Linda showed me the way. "Have you heard about the Holy Spirit?" she asked. I had not. "It's God's presence that He wants to put inside of you. It's His power, and He will give it to you if you want it. That will be the strength inside of you to become a Christian and give you the power to forgive your parents."

"How do I get it?" I asked.

"Just ask the Holy Spirit to come into your life," she replied.

I said, "Thank you very much. I'm hanging up now."

I walked across my bright blue carpet and asked the Holy Spirit to come into my life. I didn't fully understand why Jesus died on the cross for my sins. All I knew was that I should be able to honor my parents or do *something* right with them. By myself I couldn't. I knew God would give me His spirit and He would help me. It was very quiet and very powerful. I had peace. For the first time in twenty-six years, I sat down and ate an entire meal. Never before had I actually eaten and enjoyed a meal. I had always been too anxious. Later that night, as my husband and I prepared for bed, I yelled around a corner at him, "Listen, I've become a Christian, and I don't want you to ask me any questions about it."

The next morning I first called Linda, then the pastor from her church to ask for a meeting. When we met, I told him, "I asked the Holy Spirit to come into my life, and I think He has. I'm not the same person."

I did not fully understand what was happening at church, but I knew I felt safe there. I thought I needed to study, so once a week, Linda took me to a Bible Study Fellowship about forty-five miles away. All the way there and back, she talked to me of God.

I was stunned after the first Bible study lecture. The first words I learned from Jesus were: "I have come to give you life and to give it to you abundantly." I didn't know about Jacob and how he wrestled with God when I said to God, "That's what I want from You, and I will not let go of You until You give it to me."

Then I wanted everyone to learn what I had just learned. I knew from my existentialism class that I had the power to be persuasive. I prayed, "God, would You just give me a chance to persuade people to come to You? That is what I want to do."

I went to Linda and told her that God spoke to me. "I'm sure God spoke to you," she affirmed. "But God needs prepared people."

I determined to finish the existentialism class and then devote myself entirely to studying the Bible. It may have seemed presumptuous at the time, but three years later, I was teaching seven hundred women in Bible Study Fellowship.

I was growing spiritually, but I knew there was much yet

to face. My lack of sexual interest began to distress me. I read the apostle Paul's words to share your body with your husband (1 Cor. 7:3), and I did that physically, but not emotionally. I thought all women felt the way I did, but when I mentioned my lack of desire to another friend, she said, "That really isn't normal." *Is that right?* I thought to myself. She questioned me about my childhood and asked what I remembered about my father.

"Well, he walked around the house naked and drunk with a gun in his hand."

"Are you kidding?" my friend asked.

I answered no but wondered what was so unusual about that. She suggested I talk to someone qualified to help me. At the first session with a therapist, I admitted, with my husband present, that I had absolutely no sexual feelings. I had denied the images, denied the fears, denied the memories of sexual abuse for years. Now I was at a place where I had to face them.

I felt the Lord say to me, "If you want to be My disciple, you have to go through this particular door of counseling." I did want to be His disciple, and I was willing to do anything to be mature in the Lord. In recurring images, I saw myself plastered against a concrete wall, all bloody, as if I had been thrown against it. The night before I was to teach an important session for a group of women, I had a dream that a big person raped a little child in a crib. I woke up feeling sick, but I went anyway to fulfill my responsibility to teach. After the class, I returned home and faced for the first time the floating pieces of the images of being horribly violated by my father.

One night when I was absolutely frozen with pain, I went into my room and read, "Who among you fears the Lord and obeys the voice of his servant?" *Lord, that is me.* "Let him who walks in the dark, who has no light . . ." *That is me too.* An entirely new thought came to me. Previously I had thought that if you followed God, you walked in the light and you felt happy. Since I was not happy, I assumed something must be wrong. That night I realized that the error was my original thought. It was a superficial interpretation of Scripture. The real truth is that sometimes when we walk with God, we walk in darkness. "Trust in the name of the LORD and rely on his God," continues Isaiah 50:10. "Lord, I'm going to trust in who You are," I prayed. By following Him, I reached this place of darkness. And in that place, I vowed to trust Him.

God confirmed that people can act in terrible ways but that I should not confuse Him with people. When I gathered courage enough to work on the emotions I felt, I had to face my brother's abuse of me. Then I again visualized the cave incident, but this time I saw Jesus there, too, and He was weeping. Weeping for me. Weeping for those boys. I saw the difference between what people are like and what God is like. I was able to not blame God for what my father did, for what those boys did, or for my brother's behavior. I learned that God wept for my father too. I am convinced that He weeps over all sin and over every sinner.

I was greatly helped by a counselor's suggestion that I write on separate pieces of paper each of the false messages my father, my mother, and my brother gave to me, what the messages meant, and how I actually lived them out. Then, on another piece of paper, I was to write new messages, what these meant, and if possible, how I would live them out. In the relationship with my brother, one message I wrote was, "You are worthless, and you are not worth being protected." That message meant that I wasn't worthy of anything good happening to me, and I deserved to be violated. I had lived it out by putting myself in situations where people took advantage of me. Consequently I lived as a victim. My new message was "I am not worthless, and I *am* worth being protected." It meant I have value, and the things I do have value.

It took six months to identify and put into words thirteen messages from my childhood. With my husband at my side, I read a false message then the true one, now believing I could live the new message. In our fireplace, I burned thirteen old lies.

Slowly, I was able to take responsibility for my own healing. All along the way there have been incredibly important women. My grandmother. My twin, Elizabeth. Linda. There was another friend, a sister, who drove to my house during her lunch hour just to sit with me during my pain.

I learned another very important lesson. My grandfather owned a business, and my grandparents were wealthy. At one time, my husband was offered a position with their company. It would have meant financial security for the rest of our lives, even for the rest of our children's lives. But as I walked through the streets of that little town, wandered in and out of the rooms in my grandparents' house, and drove by the house where my childhood was so badly bruised, I could not justify the required exchange. No amount of money was worth returning to this place of nightmares and deliberately inflicted pain. As Jesus states in Mark 10:29–30:

"No one who has left home or brothers or sisters or mother or father or children or fields for me and the gospel will fail to receive a hundred times as much in this present age (homes, brothers, sisters, mothers, children and fields—and with them, persecutions) and in the age to come, eternal life." God did that for me. I learned that money cannot, and did not, buy safety, security, or love. Without much money, I am rich in friendships, peace, and God's love.

I will probably never live entirely free of dark and sorrowful memories of my childhood. Neither will I live without a deep gratitude for God who gave me new eyes through which I have seen beauty against darkness.

When we were little, my sister and I would try to play with my mother, only to be rebuked. I remember we once got in the car before she did and hid in the back seat. "Where is Caroline?" my mother asked. My sister giggled and said, "I don't know." My mother ended the game quickly by saying, "She never did have enough sense to get in out of the rain." Play was over. Wounds were invisible. My sister and I were both hurt by her words. But we had each other. When nothing else was reliable, my sister was. All the things we should have received from our parents, we got from each other. We investigated our world together. When parents neglected our learning and competency of skills, we encouraged each other. Even though we were very different, we were able to grow in the stability of each other's love. God supplied compensation for what our parents lacked, and we gave hope to each other. We gave each other skills. We nursed wounds and sympathized with each other's scars. We were sisters in a world where we didn't have anyone else.

The Story Goes On

To some people, scars are ugly. They are embarrassing reminders of foolish or traumatic events. Scars are often painful reminders of tragedy. Some try to hide their scars, as if to mask their sorrow or shame. Others may expose or flaunt scars as a trophy of triumph or to shock. For all, a scar signifies a painful experience, whether brief, like that of my young son, or decades long, like that of Caroline.

Abuse is too small a word to describe the destruction of a child at the hands of her parents. Courage is too quiet a word to describe how Caroline escaped being hardened by her scars. She has not been made harsh or unapproachable. In her case, dreadful wounds are healing into marks of self-acceptance and connectedness to others. On this new path of life, Christ lovingly heals her darkest memories and leads her to the redemption of even her childhood losses.

Not all women survive with the same results. One woman's words were "I have forgiven my father," but as she spoke, her head hung down, her shoulders stooped, her hands were tightly clasped, and hot tears rolled down her face. Another woman who spoke to me could not tell her story; to relive the events of her abuse was too great an emotional price, even for the sake of her sisters. Some women are not far enough through their stories yet. The wounds are still too tender and not totally healed.

For sisters like Caroline, we who listen either ignite hope or we arrest healing by denying, minimizing, or ignoring their pain. Think about this: Scarring, whether of a body, a mind, or the emotions, is mostly an ugly process *but* it does wonderfully good work at the site of the wound. When healing begins, a scab forms to prevent further infection. As restoration works underneath a scab, scar tissue thickens, and it literally gets tough. It is as if the body fortifies itself against further injury to the same location. By wise and active compassion, we can encourage the wounded back to healthy toughness, to strength without rigidity, and back to God, our trustworthy Father.

But I will restore you to health and heal your wounds, declares the LORD.   JEREMIAH 30:17

Don't Hide the Scars

I wept all alone
suffered on my own
I didn't think that anyone would understand
until you opened up
and shared your painful past with me
Then the wounds that I kept hidden
were touched by heaven's hand
because God used you
and all that you've been through

Chorus:
Don't hide the scars
Don't be afraid to let them show
'Cause someone who hurts will see herself in you
There's healing in knowing you're not the only one
You can touch another heart
Don't hide the scars

Everyone must go
through dark nights of the soul
and bear the pain and all the wounds
that life can bring
For in those worst of times
we need the strength of another
With God's love flowing through her
we find the faith we need
So no matter where we've stood
It all works out for good[8]

10

Abandonment:
A Woman's Sorrow,
A Child's Fear

---

*"I have never really understood my
mother's need to send me away."*

Loréss (not her real name) and I are sisters. Not by birth, but by choice. Photographs of us, arms wrapped around each other's waist, show our physical differences. My long, straight brown hair frames my pale skin. A mass of braids dangle around Loréss's luminous light brown sugar skin. Her eyes tease when she calls herself a "Nubian princess."

Photographs cannot capture our similarities. Both of us are strong-willed and determined, much to the dismay of some of our business associates. Both of us are emotionally tender and weep upon hearing of another's pain. We have a similar desire to know God as a loving Father and to avoid feeling the detachment of our own alcoholic fathers. Both of us know the pain of abandonment by someone we love, and we both carry the self-inflicted pain born of poor choices.

Loréss's Story

My mother's family is from New York and my father's family is from North Carolina. I was told my father's German surname was given to his ancestors by slave owners. I was born in the Bronx. My parents divorced when I was about two and my paternal grandmother came up from North Carolina to take me home with her. I have never really understood my mother's need to send me away.

I grew up in North Carolina among wonderful, spiritual women: my great-grandmother, my grandmother (whom I lovingly called Momma Essie), her sisters, and my great-aunts. As the first great-granddaughter, I was loved and spoiled. My earliest memories are filled with summer: picking tobacco and cotton, catching fish, rabbit, and squirrel, climbing trees, running in open fields, splashing my warm bare feet in icy creeks. The highlight of the day was bathing in a huge outdoor tub. Thirteen cousins lined up for a dunk in the water, waited for a vigorous drying off, then raced up the stairs of a huge old house to jump between stiff, clean sheets. I can still smell the ever-present aroma of cookies and pies baking in the oven. I remember watching aunts fashion Sunday hats and sew dresses by hand. I was happy, secure, and loved. I was home.

This carefree reign ended when I was ten years old. My mother, whom I called Momma Joyce on her infrequent visits, and my father, whom she had recently remarried, arrived in North Carolina with my new brother. They packed me up and moved me with them back to the projects of New York City. All that was familiar was gone. In the city, I fell asleep to the sounds of cars, buses, and trains. My playground was concrete. In place of twelve playful cousins, I had only my infant brother.

My mother and father, virtual strangers to me, worked during the day. At night, my father drank. When he arrived home, the arguing began, screaming followed, and the end came with the beatings. My father did not limit his battering to my mother. My brother and I often were included in his violent outbursts. Lying in bed with the blanket over my head, I begged God to protect us all. "Please," I prayed. "Don't let anything bad happen." Lying awake at night, I plotted and planned an escape. My childish mind cringed and folded before the scenes I so frequently witnessed: my father pummeling my mother, my mother cowering, my father staggering into bed, my mother jerking my bedcovers off to accuse me of not helping her. I promised myself I would never live my adult life in this way.

A few months after my move, my beloved grandmother, Momma Essie, came to New York. She visited our house briefly before going to her sister's. Then, a few days later, my father came home early. I was sent to my room, but I could hear my parents crying and whispering. "What are you going to tell her?" I overheard. Finally they told me that Momma Essie, the mother of my heart, had died. I was taken to the funeral home to see the cold, motionless figure in the coffin. It in no way resembled my warm, vibrant grandmother. *That's not Momma,* I remember thinking to myself. I felt truly alone, truly abandoned.

When I was twelve, as unexpectedly as I had been moved to New York, my parents became Seventh Day Adventist Christians. Family worship, traditionally reserved for Sunday, moved to Saturday. Pork and red meats were replaced with vegetarian protein. Though I embraced the healthiness of our new denomination, it represented yet another loss of my familiar past.

Soon after this, my father read in an Adventist magazine that families were better off living in the country. He announced our upcoming move, and again the familiar and secure was ripped away. Our move to a little town where the majority of the residents were white served up the worst year of my life.

I finished my first year of junior high in our new town. Then my parents decided I should attend an Adventist boarding school twelve hours away. My regularly being sent away was by now indelibly imprinted on my soul. Time never permitted a feeling of safety or belonging. The relentless pattern of abandonment seared my psyche—and stirred up anger. Anger that once again my mother sent me away. Anger that my beloved grandmother died. Anger that my violent father intruded into my life. Anger that I lived without a sense of permanence.

The adjustment from the North Carolina farm to the city of New York little prepared me for the adjustment from an all-black elementary school in the city to an all-white boarding school in the country. Trying to find my place and trying to raise myself, I entered my teenage years like any girl does—listening to music, giggling, and applying makeup. Using my white classmates' foundation, I turned a comically seasick shade of gray.

Against all odds, I was successful at school. I was president of both the Girls' Club and our Saturday afternoon youth meetings. Since I wasn't interested in dating any boy for our version of the prom, I threw myself into the staging and decorating. We turned the gymnasium into a pillared Victorian estate and covered the entire floor with fake grass. For the Christmas shows, I dressed up my friends like toys and made them jump out of decorated boxes. And, for reasons that escape me, I was the resident counselor. Anyone with a problem came to me. I felt important when my advice caused a girl to respond with "That's it! That's exactly right!"

Self-inflicted pressure to be somebody was very intense. I needed to belong but I didn't let anyone get too close. Fellow students told me their problems, but I didn't tell them mine. Cautious and reserved, I was never sure how to show need or affection. After the death of my dear grandmother, I had never again felt the touch of a tender hand, never caught the smiling eyes of a proud parent, or sensed that I was loved.

In contrast to my North Carolina grandparents, my mother's parents were stereotypical New Yorkers. My grandmother was a pioneering fashion-industry buyer and a socialite, elegant and proper. She bestowed on me a sense of fashion and a flair for decorating. During Christmas and holidays, I usually returned to her home in New York City. But most of my summer and spring breaks were spent in church camps as either a camper or a counselor. I lived my teen years totally separated from a family system. When I grew up, I wanted a home like the one I knew in North Carolina.

In my senior year of high school, I was chosen Most Likely to Succeed. Because most of my teachers, counselors, and friends said, "You would make the perfect minister's wife," and to distance myself even farther from my family, I decided to go to Lincoln, Nebraska, to an Adventist college. I didn't want to be a minister's wife; I wanted to be a missionary. I had to make it clear to the faculty that I didn't want to be a missionary's *wife*, I wanted to *be* the missionary. I was stunned and saddened to hear that neither black males nor black females were sent overseas as missionaries. Another dream, another hope, was taken away from me.

There were few black students at college, and unfortunately, the most popular black male did not at all impress me. He was boisterous, flamboyant, loud, funny, and the center of everything. All the guys and all the girls, everyone white and black, adored him. Except me. But, human nature being what it is, winning me over became his mission.

During our sophomore year, he attended a different school in another state and we found ourselves writing friendly, nonromantic letters to each other. During my junior year, he returned to Nebraska and our relationship changed. His theatrical behavior thinly camouflaged his insecurity and encouraged my blossoming codependency. *I can help him*, I thought.

When the time came to make decisions about marriage, I had no reference point for making good choices. I was twenty-one. It was "time" to marry and before I could stop it, I walked down the aisle thinking, *Someone should stop us from doing this*. In an attempt to bridge the gap she and I straddled, my mother spent a lot of time and money to make mine a storybook wedding.

It soon became evident that what was once charming in my husband was really dangerously erratic behavior stemming from a combination of issues in his life. After two years, our daughter was born. My pregnancy was very difficult, but when Reneé (not her real name) arrived, she became my life. She was the only joy in my sad little home. The first time my husband and I separated, I flew to my grandmother's house. My parents phoned me there, hysterically screaming into the receiver, "How could you do this to us?" I had no idea what they were talking about. "Why didn't you come home?" my mother demanded. Only then did I realize that home was not where my birth parents lived. There was only, ever, one home for me—in North Carolina, with my beloved grandmother, aunts, uncles, and cousins.

After several separations and several attempts to salvage the marriage, it finally failed. After a year alone as a divorced mother of a toddler, I attended a week-long revival meeting to hear a well-known Adventist speaker. Toward the end of the week, I was introduced to one of the singers in the musical group who traveled with the speaker. Ronald (not his real name) seemed spiritually connected, strong, and confident. On stage, he was an energetic, exciting performer. Off stage, he appeared shy and childlike. Something clicked and we began an eighteen-month, long-distance, letter-writing relationship.

Along with this new romantic interest, my relationship with my mother was developing. We finally had something in common: divorce and remarriage. Now we met as two adult women, not as a mother and daughter. Every Sunday morning we talked on the phone, and she began writing letters. "I know you are worried about me," she wrote in reference to her relationship with my father, "and I love you all the more for it. You must not worry about two people who should be able to manage their conduct. You must conduct your own life." *Good advice,* I thought, *but how do I do that?*

It is hard to admit to a second wrong marriage. Under the pressure of families and against my own instincts, that is what I did. Ronald wrongly thought his love for me was enough for both of us, but that, of course, is never true. Doubting my own judgment, but wanting to please others, I walked down the aisle for the second time. I think now I married because when I admitted my fear, my father was furious and belligerent. I was afraid of his judgment and of Ronald's potential abandonment.

Two weeks after the wedding, we moved to Nashville, Tennessee. As was so familiar in my life, I was left alone. Ronald was on the road almost constantly during our first year of marriage, and I was alone in a strange town.

The rapid succession of years blurred with joy and pain. My son was born. My maternal grandfather and my mother died. This was not just my mother I was burying; she was my new friend. I was thirty-three years old and only beginning to understand her pain; then I had to choose burial clothes, write an obituary, and bury her. My sense of abandonment soared. Knowing no way to verbalize my deep feelings, I suppressed my pain. Now when I needed grief, it, too, abandoned me.

Around this time, a singing group of young men from an Adventist college approached me to ask if I knew any management companies and booking agencies in Nashville. I did. Together we sent out their tapes and photographs. I arranged meetings for them, but our attempts proved futile.

In my busyness, I had volunteered to work for the Urban League and the Metro Arts Commission, which organized a citywide summer concert. I served on the committee for gospel music night and saw a chance to give those boys a break. So I added them to the list of performers and set up a showcase in a local Christian bookstore, to which both secular and Christian record company executives were invited. Within twenty-four hours after the showcase, a secular record executive offered a contract to the group. We were astounded and thrilled! I reluctantly agreed to attend the first meeting with the record company. Afterward, I suggested they needed a good attorney, but, to my astonishment, they insisted on my involvement. From that moment, my life changed. I worked tirelessly, and within a few years, the group gathered multiple Grammy and Dove awards, international media coverage, and out-and-out acclaim from the entertainment world.

Accolades for my business sense appeared in the form of statuettes, plaques, and framed commendations. I was getting a lot of attention from strangers. Sadly, the distance between Ronald and me widened. Communication became difficult, especially about things happening with the group. My success seemed liked pouring salt into his wound since our move to Nashville was for *his* career. I didn't even *have* a career. Now, in a just a few years and by accident, I was taking phone calls from famous people, from producers and artists I had admired or read about in newspapers and magazines. They were calling *me* to negotiate record deals, national commercials, and movie appearances. Calls were coming in for clothing endorsements, magazine spreads, and charity appearances.

Guilt also called: Why was I working so hard for these young men I barely knew? Because it appealed to all of me:

my maternal, creative, controlling, codependent parts. It kept me busy and away from the truth of my loneliness and crumbling marriage. My high school and college prayers to be used by God seemed answered in this way. I tried to include Ronald in my work. He wrote a review of the group for *Billboard* magazine and even accompanied the guys to some concert dates. However, the distance between us grew so great that he refused to go places with me. I stopped asking for his time. The group became more successful, and I became busier. I hired help for children and house care. Ronald and I grew more distant.

Surely friends and associates noticed that I attended concerts and award ceremonies alone, but no one asked why. I know my outward demeanor suggested control and everyone assumed I was fine. The ever-tightening noose of our failing marriage nearly strangled me, but I kept my problems buried. I didn't know how to ask for help and people didn't offer it. I felt abandoned.

My terrified determination to survive suggested that I was strong. Unknowingly, I pushed people away. They got the message that I didn't need them, but I did—desperately. In every situation in my life, I expected people to leave me, to abandon me. By my desperate habits, I saw to it that they did.

I grew tired—tired of working double-duty shifts, of bearing the responsibility for my husband, my children, my home, the group, and for my office, and tired of my isolated heart. The Enemy knew my weakness. He knew my longing for validation and love had not changed since I was shipped to New York, since age fourteen when I was handed to a boarding school and abandoned by my family.

It is not unusual for bad to get worse. It did. I met a man who valued my work and my abilities. I absorbed his compliments like dry desert sand drinks water. So great was my need for affection, affirmation, and human touch that I dismissed the voice of God and the voice of guilt ringing in my ears.

I do not know how common it is, but Ronald and I had grown so distant that we both fell into the sin of adultery. We separated. I blamed Ronald for his affair, and I blamed him for mine. Finally, with great reluctance, I listened to the insistent command of the Holy Spirit to leave the arms of a man not my husband. Ronald and I tried to apologize to each other, but my guilt made me harsh and judgmental. Occasionally, I wanted to reconcile but Ronald didn't. When he wanted to work it out, I was indifferent.

It is hard to admit now, and it was hard to comprehend then, that my second marriage was ending in divorce. My guilt continued to grow intolerably. I went to my pastor and asked for help. He surmised that lingering guilt was eating me up, emotionally and physically. To convince me that my iniquity could be forgiven, he took me into the church sanctuary for baptism. How wise he was. A sinful yet repentant Loréss submerged; the forgiven Loréss rose. The symbolic act of washing away sin was for me reality. But the damage of sin was not so easily removed. I had an enormous amount of maturing ahead.

Before the divorce, I let my closest friends see my successes, awards, and other good things. After the divorce, I let them see all of me, including the mistakes, the pain, and the hurt. Jae was the first sister to hear the nightmare of my life. She cried with me over the phone. She didn't like what

I had done or what had been done to me, but she cried with me. Marie (not her real name) was the next sister to whom I confessed the state of my life. I thought I sounded okay during our Tuesday phone conversation, but she heard the pain in my voice. On Friday she arrived on my doorstep. "I am here to cook, to clean, to do whatever you need." She brought a stack of books about something called codependency. I had never heard of it. *Great!* I thought. *There's a name for these crazy emotions I feel!*

For the first time, at the lowest point of my failures, I discovered the joy of supportive friends. My friend Rhonda called me every morning at 7:30 A.M. to pray. "Please heal my sister," she asked. I learned what an intercessor was. Rhonda carried my burden to the Lord for me and with me. She was the first to read me Joel 2:25–26: "I will repay you for the years the locusts have eaten. . . . You will have plenty to eat, until you are full, and you will praise the name of the LORD your God, who has worked wonders for you; never again will my people be shamed."

"The years the locusts have eaten" represented my lost childhood, the years of abandonment, lost feelings of love, and my lifetime of a kind of homelessness. "You will have plenty to eat" was fulfilled as God surrounded me with women who were comfortable with themselves. Women who had grown up in dysfunctional homes like mine and who understood emptiness. Women who survived crisis and loss yet remained emotionally stable. Through friends, old and young, God restored to me gentle, tender, nurturing care. Friends I had known all my life came back to me, and God sent in a whole new army of women to assist in the rebuilding of my life. "Never again will my people be shamed" meant me. I *was* ashamed of my behavior, my divorces, of me. I had hoped against hope to ever hold my head up in real strength, in true health, and in the confidence of Christ. Now I was surrounded by helping, healthy friends.

My dear friend Debbie brought me a cassette tape of a preacher who quoted a verse that became a turning point in my life: "Woman, you are set free from your infirmity" (Luke 13:12). My infirmity bulged conspicuously: my loss of family, loss of belonging, feelings of loneliness and abandonment, my homelessness. I wanted to be free. I wanted to laugh again. I wanted to be loved.

Over the last few years, those longings have turned to realities. Evidence of this healing surfaced recently when a friend of mine asked if his mother could accompany me on a trip to Los Angeles. I agreed, thinking I would be responsible for her entertainment and happiness. Little did I know.

Juanita loves life. She is inquisitive and energetic and, I soon learned, a lot of fun. Once, when a few of Juanita's distant family members came to pick her up from our hotel, she introduced me with pride, like I was her daughter. We went shopping and she helped me choose a dress to wear to the Grammys. We shared girl talk: makeup, clothes, perfume. We discussed our children. We talked and giggled late into the night. We shared that neither of us had our mothers and how we both missed them.

As a music professional, I am often numb to the glitz and glamour in the industry. But Juanita's excitement was contagious. Sitting in the Grammy audience, she was thrilled by the presence of people she had heard on the radio, seen on television, or read about in magazines. When highly recognized artists walked by, she nearly flew out of her chair.

When Deniece Williams came to our hotel room that day, Juanita leapt off the bed, overjoyed to meet the artist whose voice she knew as Niecé. We went to the home of actress Hattie Winston, and Juanita shrieked, "I remember you from *The Electric Company! I* saw you in *Beverly Hills Cop III!*" We laughed with her at her unrestrained delight.

The night before the Grammys, I received a Congressional Music Award. During my acceptance speech, Juanita's eyes shone with pride; they never left my face. When I returned to my seat, I handed the award to her. I had been escorted to other award shows, but never had I experienced such emotion and support. She was proud of me—like a mother. No other look compares to that of a mother's, and for that instant the gift was mine.

On the flight home, Juanita wrote fast and furiously in her journal. She wanted to record every detail of our trip to California—everything she did, everyone she met—so she could tell her teenage granddaughters. As we approached Nashville, she started to cry.

"What's wrong, Juanita?" I asked.

"I'll never be able to thank you," she replied.

It was my turn to cry. "No, I'll never be able to thank you," I confessed. "I never shared any of this with my mother. She never shared a hotel room with me, or went to the Grammys with me, or held my purse while I spoke, or saw any of my awards."

I told Juanita about a letter my mother sent to me a few years before she died: "It's so hot here in New York," she wrote. "I wish I was near some water, lying on the sand, feeling the cool breeze off the water." One day on the trip, Juanita had asked to go to the beach, and I'd taken her. We spent a whole day there together, next to water, feeling the breeze. God restored what had been eaten away in my life. God gave me a woman like a mother. In ten days, we built a love that ought to require ten years to form.

What a sight Juanita and I probably were as we worked to regain our composure: two African-American women clinging to each other at 37,000 feet. "No matter what happens," Juanita said, "I will always be here for you." My soul had waited half my life to hear such words from a mother: a promise never to leave me or abandon me.

The Story Goes On

When Loréss told me her story, I wept as she painfully unfolded the details. Often we sat in silence for many minutes, recovering from the sorrow of her abandonment and homelessness. Looking into her face, I caught a glimpse of the scared little girl trembling with fear in her bed.

Loréss is quick to take responsibility for her actions. She read a very important sentence to me: "When we fail to listen to God, others around us are hurt."[9] The consequences of her life choices did not affect just her. "Two failed marriages and an affair and not knowing who I was, or where I belonged, in my eyes lessened my value. I want desperately to not diminish the value of the people with whom I made the mistakes. They are God's people."

God does value Loréss, and she is learning that. He is taking her brokenness, her mistakes, and her failures and transforming them into strengths and wisdom. Looking back, a single thread weaves through all the torn, frayed pieces of her life and ties her past to her present. The thread is her story. A story of restoration she has no choice but to tell—for the sake of others and for the healing of her heart.

Sometimes now, when she laughs, I catch a glimpse of a barefoot little girl, skipping in the North Carolina grass. In Loréss's new peace, she is home.

On a Sabbath Jesus was teaching in one of the synagogues, and a woman was there who had been crippled by a spirit for eighteen years. She was bent over and could not straighten up at all. When Jesus saw her, he called her forward and said to her, "Woman, you are set free from your infirmity." Then he put his hands on her, and immediately she straightened up and praised God. LUKE 13:10–13

11

Mistakes and Sin:
Women Experience Them; Wise Women Help Women Who Do

---

*"I have heard God is a stickler for
obedience and good behavior; but I have
also heard He is a forgiver of sin."*

Opinions on the issue of abortion stretch from righteous damnation to rigorous political rights. Caught in the middle are women. A woman's choice is not merely whether or not to have a child. Choices include whether to tell or not to tell.

When young Marla (not her real name) found herself considering abortion, no one came alongside her. She was one who chose not to tell. No one offered comfort. No one gave her hope for the future. In the quietness of her own soul she asked for, and received, forgiveness. When she finally did risk sharing her whole experience, her courage got slapped with startling and discouraging results.

Marla's Story

In my first year of college, I met the tall, dark, and handsome man of my dreams. His intelligence, humor, and talent opened up a whole new world to me. I loved him.

We were Christians, and we were young. And we were passionate. We tried our best to be "good." We tried to be responsible. For over a year, we abstained from sex. But the night finally came when our desire outweighed our intent. Yielding to each other was glorious. We held each other tightly. We cried. We whispered "I love you" over and over. Neither of us wanted to let go of each other or the evening. Our love was forever. I was happy.

Then I proved the medical fact that you can get pregnant the first time you have sex. When my suspicions were confirmed, my feelings vacillated between happiness and fear, joy and anger. When I phoned my boyfriend, who lived in another state, his response was the same as my own: "What are we going to do?" How common this question is—until it belongs to you.

I sat in a church service, eighteen years old and pregnant, and knew that I had to make a choice. But how do you make a decision of that magnitude? I wondered what others would do in my place.

I looked over at my parents. They had invested a lot of money in my piano and voice lessons, college tuition, and future. "Make something of yourself," my dad had told me. "Don't get married until you graduate from college and have a career. Don't depend on a man to take care of you. Be independent."

What would they choose? My pregnancy would disappoint them. They would feel shame for my failure. I dreaded hearing "How could you do this?"

My generation, now called baby boomers, was encouraged and pushed to succeed. Succeed in school: "Get a college education." Succeed in business: "Work hard; climb that corporate ladder." Succeed financially: "Be secure; invest wisely; buy a house." Succeed individually: "Be independent; be self-sufficient; be happy." Succeed spiritually: "Be ye Holy, as I am Holy." Succeed personally: "Don't mess up your life." Not only does our American culture encourage success above all, but our Christian culture does too.

What was my spiritual choice? I looked at the adults seated around me in pews and observed that this congregation possessed everything money could buy. They appeared well dressed and mannerly. Successful. Spiritual. They also flaunted everything superiority buys. Judgment. Gossip. Snideness. They displayed much. Pride. Power. Affluence.

A few things were not readily available among these, my older fellow Christians. Compassion. Forgiveness. Love. *How would they react,* I mused, *if they knew I was pregnant? Me, the talented one. The outgoing one. The leader of the youth group?*

I knew. Sorrowfully, I knew. The way they had with the other "sinners" in the church—with gossip and harshness. Perhaps, had I been older, I could have challenged prevailing attitudes. At age eighteen I *heard* about grace but *watched* a spirit of intolerance.

I looked at my pastor. What would he say? How would he respond if he knew? Would he be different from his congregation? Would he be more compassionate? Would he help me find a way to give birth to the child and allow adoption?

I thought about my boyfriend. What was his choice? He wasn't emotionally or financially ready to be a father, he said. He wanted to be a good daddy, but later, when the proper time came. And to be a good daddy he had to finish college and make something of his life. And, oh yes, make a lot of money.

What was my choice? Who would know if I had an abortion? Two people? Three or four, if you include a doctor and a nurse? How bad could it be? The doctor thought of my pregnancy as only a wad of tissue at this point. A counselor said to think of my own life. My boyfriend said to think of our future. My church said to keep up outward appearances. My family said to succeed.

I did not know what God said. This "sin" was not a regular pulpit or Sunday school class topic so many years ago. I did not know if God had an opinion. I *did* know that He was a stickler for obedience and "good" behavior; but I also heard that He was a forgiver of sin.

Where would I go? In those days there were no pregnancy crisis centers. I had no extended family members. I felt I had no options. I made what I thought was the all-around best decision. Best—which probably amounted to easiest—for my boyfriend, my parents, my church, and my future. I would be the one to carry the guilt, the secret. Who, besides myself, would suffer? I did not allow myself to think of the baby.

After my abortion in one of the only legal clinics in California, I saw my boyfriend only a few times. The tension was too great between us. My mother found out about the abortion by discovering some pills in my purse. Her anger included the phrase, "How could you do this to me?" And, as I expected, her main concern was that no one know. We never again discussed it.

That does not mean that my mother did not discuss it, however. She apparently confided to our pastor that she was worried about me and my relationships. The next time he saw me, he closed me in a very tight embrace. When I struggled to release myself from his grasp, he held me even closer, saying, "Come on, I know what kind of girl you are."

I cried until I couldn't cry anymore. I thought more and more about what I had done. The deed could not be undone, and my life had to go on even as I faced having stopped another's. I begged God for His forgiveness, and I received it.

A few months later, my parents and I were visiting in a friend's home. Sitting in a bedroom with their teenage daughter, Gina (not her real name), I questioned her obvious sadness.

"I had an abortion a few days ago," Gina replied tearfully. I listened to a pained account of her realization of pregnancy, her parents' horrified reaction, and their insistence on an abortion. Her own father drove her to the clinic.

I realized Gina was bleeding emotionally. Remembering my own mother's scorching words, I opted to guide Gina to the way of peace and forgiveness.

"Gina," I whispered, "I know how you feel. I had an abortion not long ago. But if we ask Him, Jesus Christ offers forgiveness for all our sins. He wants to live in us and give us a new start." I explained that God gives us hope for the future. If I believed this to be true for myself, then it had to be true for Gina. I prayed for Gina and myself. We both felt His forgiveness.

I knew right then that God could use me to help girls who had made the same choice. I was eager to tell my story since I saw it helped bring healing. I was not prepared for the disaster that followed. Gina's mother called my mother the next day. "So, I hear you have skeletons in your closet."

"What are you talking about?" my mother asked.

"Gina told me that Marla had an abortion too."

Fury met me at home after school that day. "What did you think you were doing, telling Gina?" my mother raged.

"I prayed with her," I shot back. "Isn't that the point of being a Christian—telling others there is forgiveness for *every* sin? Even mine?"

My mother did not readily share that viewpoint. Her reputation filled her mind. I saw my experience as a platform to help others, but the blastings of my mother represented to me what all Christians believed: Keep it to yourself. My shame centered not on my action, but on the telling of it. Since that day until now, I have not told anyone else that I had an abortion. I've kept my little secret.

Recently, I attended a luncheon with three other Christian women. The topic of abortion provoked animated gestures and passionate conversation. Opinions blew between us concerning the responsibility of the church versus education in the public schools, private payment for abortion versus government funding, effectiveness of crisis pregnancy centers, and the evils of Planned Parenthood.

They don't have a clue, I thought to myself. *Not one of them truly knows or understands the emotion a woman feels when she realizes she is unwillingly pregnant.*

I was jolted back from my thoughts when I heard one of the women say, "I don't know what kind of a woman would have an abortion."

I was aghast. *What kind of a woman?* My thoughts were a whirlwind of searing hurt and sadness. *What kind of a woman?* How isolated from the real world *is* the woman who spoke those words? Does she not know even one woman who has chosen to abort a baby? She may not think she knows one, but they are present in her life. She just doesn't know it.

I knew the answer to her inquiry. *Every* kind of woman. Single. Married. Young. Old. Selfish. Generous. Rich. Poor. Catholic. Evangelical. Terrified. Betrayed. Trapped.

My reeling thoughts collided with my frantic emotions. How could I verbalize the rush of words racing through my mind? I wanted to scream, "I had an abortion when I was eighteen years old. What do you think of *me* now?"

I forced my attention back to the conversation. The three were still waxing wise about women who aren't responsible enough to use birth control, or strong enough to exert self-control, or, or, or . . .

I asked the Lord to help me express myself without judging my friends, without causing harm, and without anger.

Finding the courage to speak, I began, "I think differently from the rest of you. We need to look at Jesus' example with the woman at the well. He did not quote condemning Scripture to her. He did not start a divorce recovery group in her town. He took the time to sit and have a glass of water with her. He did not dwell on the issue of her past behavior, but helped her see her future.

"I do not feel that, as Christians, we have the right to condemn women who sought abortions. They were not always offered a true alternative, so why do we judge their response to what seems their only option? Screaming at women in front of clinics or shooting doctors is not a very loving way to invite a woman to sit and have a glass of water."

The Story Goes On

As a Christian sister to women like Marla, I very much need to respect her story. Marla is now married and has children. But in group discussions about abortion, she never says a word. As she listens to energetic discussions around her, the old question still circles in her mind: *What would they say if they knew?*

"The church really doesn't offer forgiveness, does it?" Marla asked me. "If you are sick and then healed, you're expected never to mention your sickness again. It was so confusing to me as a teenager to read the verse that says 'Jesus came to heal the sick.' I knew that was me. Yet in my Sunday school class, the teachers condemned 'loose girls' and 'hippie boys.' How can we present salvation to our friends if we don't tell them the truth and show the forgiveness of Christ in our lives?"

The Holy Spirit freed Marla to tell her own experience; her mother condemned the same action. The guilt she felt in the following years was not nearly so much over the actual abortion as for admitting it.

Like Marla, in the 1970s singer/songwriter Julie Miller had an abortion. Later, as she realized the sad truth of what abortion means, she embraced Christ and His forgiveness.

She, too, found the freedom needed to tell her story for the sake of other young women. "If anyone can be forgiven, we all can," she said. "I think recovering from abortion is a lifelong thing, but God has brought me to a place where it is a sorrow, not a torment. There is also the hope that God will, in the end, redeem it all. That I'll see my lost child, and I'll be fully restored within my own soul. Eventually, the healing will be complete."

Marla found the peace with God that Julie describes, but the same peace with fellow believers eludes her. Afraid that women friends will react as her mother did, when the topic arises among Christian women, Marla swallows her story. She knows the Lord's forgiveness, and she knows that He "will remember their sins no more" (Jer. 31:34), but she fears that mothers, and some sisters, may remember it forever.

If we are truly pro-life, we must support and protect the people outside the womb as well as those within it. Especially will we protect young women who face the quandaries confronting Marla.

If we want to offer women a workable alternative to abortion, we must support organizations that actually *do* something rather than only *say* something. Under the direction of Nancy Alcorn, Mercy Ministries in Nashville, Tennessee, has created a loving environment for young women facing such things as unplanned pregnancies, substance abuse, and emotional problems. Mercy Ministries provides a place to live, a place to sort out options, as well as spiritual guidance and emotional healing.

In the New Testament, Christians were noted for their love. Today, we are more often known for our rigidity. Knowing Marla and the response she received from Christians, I long to see the church return to the role of being a refuge, a place where frightened women can run for help. The church must provide forgiveness and tangible aid to women with unplanned pregnancies. It must be a place where women are accepted in the arms of people who aim at their futures, not their pasts.

If we truly understand God's love, we who can will tell the story that may change the life of some suffering woman. We will, without criticism, accept the women among us who saw abortion as their only way through a threatening situation. Ours is to teach but not condemn. We must assume what Jesus assumes: that any woman touched by the healing, forgiving hand of God is truly forgiven. Many of them are among us as loving wives, devoted mothers, compassionate friends, and reflections of Christ. Nothing less.

In *Jesus According to a Woman*, Rachel Conrad Wahlberg wrote about tough situations for women. The experience of the adulterous woman who was flung at the feet of the Savior caused her to highlight this response:

> For nineteen centuries Christendom has resounded with sermons on the admonition, "Go and sin no more." But rarely have sermons or ethical teachings been based on Jesus' first judgment, "Neither do I condemn you."
> And it is a judgment. To be judgmental is usually given a negative connotation. But Jesus here gave a judgment that was not negative but positive. He says he does not condemn the woman for what the community was condemning her. *He gave a freeing judgment.*
> Why has one saying been heard but not the other? I believe that the forgiveness, the non-condemning quality

of his position, is so unthinkable—so unrelated to most churchgoers' attitudes, that people have never accepted it.

. . . Christian men and women have not accepted the breakthrough challenge to responsibility: *Let him who is without sin cast the first stone.* Or the liberating sentence: *Neither do I condemn you.*[10]

"Then neither do I condemn you," Jesus declared. "Go and leave your life of sin."   JOHN 8:11

12

Faith:

Some Women Wait for Women Who Do Not

"People are not brought into the kingdom just by your being their friend."

Jim and I have been Nancy's friends for twenty-six years. We cherish the privilege of sharing in so many events of her life. When she was naturalized as a United States citizen, we proudly grinned as she pledged her allegiance. During the months of her pregnancy, we mercilessly teased her about her ever-expanding girth. Our love for her and our interest in her Polish heritage prompted our visit to Poland. We wept with her over the death of her father and then her mother.

Nancy welcomes people into her life and home as if they were family. And before long, they *are* family. When, for a few years, we lived across the street from her, we were often in each other's homes, borrowing ingredients, sharing meals, loving each other's children. We also worked in the same office, and there we were impressed by her dedication and work ethic.

Nancy's natural confidence frees her to share life's valuable lessons with her friends. However, with her friend Cathy she once remained uncharacteristically silent. She tells her story here because she feels a lesson can be learned by her Christian sisters.

Nancy's Story

I was surrounded by Christians. My full-time work was with a Christian organization, I was very active in my church, and most of my neighbors were Christians. Feeling a desire to share my faith with non-Christians, I prayed, "Lord, bring me into contact with people who might benefit from my knowing You."

The Lord answered this prayer by first answering another one. For many years my husband, Ken, and I tried to conceive a child. When against all odds I became pregnant, we joined a Lamaze birth group. At our last session, the instructor suggested we mothers form a support group after the babies' births. It wasn't until the third time we met that I realized, *Aha! The Lord has answered* both *of my prayers!*

As time passed, five of us from the class stuck together and met monthly with our babies. Before long we got smart and decided to leave our babies with their dads and have a night out alone. On these occasions, our conversations generally centered around our children. We sometimes talked of spiritual ideas, but rarely did our conversation get really deep. I wasn't overt in telling my story or giving my personal testimony.

Our friendships developed through the months and years, additional children were born, and our husbands became involved in our social outings. We took vacations and week-end trips together, shared babies' clothes and cribs, and commiserated about our lack of sleep and the realities of parenting. Through it all, Ken and I were honest about our faith and how it affected our opinions and outlook on life. Our involvement with the church and our commitment to our Christian work were no secret.

As these families became more interwoven and the adults became intimate friends, conversations covered almost any subject, including spiritual issues. In discussions of creation and evolution, religion and politics, and other potentially volatile topics that only good friends dare discuss, Ken and I stated who we believe God is, who Jesus is, but never did we say, "Here is how to receive Christ." I realize now the great difference between talking about spiritual things and letting people know you are a believer in Christ. *Talking about* doesn't get people into the kingdom. You have to be more specific. I learned that truth from Cathy.

Cathy knew one other Christian besides me, a coworker in her real estate office who was overt about her faith: "I just sold a house. Praise the Lord!" Cathy told me that the staff laughed at Margaret's (not her real name) religious outbursts.

Cathy was having difficulties in her marriage and she was planning to confront her husband about their relationship. She asked me if, under the circumstances, her daughter could spend the night in our home.

"Of course," was my reply. Then I added, "Tomorrow is Sunday; would you mind if we took her to church with us?"

"That would be fine," Cathy agreed. Then she surprised

me completely. "Maybe I will come to church too." Never before had she expressed any interest in attending our church.

The music had just begun when Cathy slipped into the seat next to me. We greeted each other with a smile and turned our attention to the platform. During the service she seemed obviously uncomfortable. I remember she squirmed and appeared impatient. I thought, *Oh, no, she hates it*. At the end of the service, she and I exchanged a quick hug, then went to retrieve our daughters from Sunday school.

That afternoon, I answered my phone only to hear Cathy on the line. "Could we have lunch tomorrow?" she requested.

"Of course," I replied, sure that she was going to tell me how much she hated church.

Sitting across the table from her the next day at lunch, I bravely asked Cathy how she enjoyed the service. "It seemed strange to me. I really didn't like it, but I want to go again," she answered. My surprised expression led Cathy to explain.

"Last night, I called Margaret to discuss some real estate business. The conversation turned to personal matters when I mentioned that I was at my wit's end with my husband. 'I know you are a Christian,' I said to Margaret. 'I wish you would pray for him; he needs help.'"

My eyes widened as Cathy related the next part of their phone conversation. "Margaret said to me, 'I think we need to pray for you and get you straightened out.'

"So," Cathy continued, "last night over the telephone, I prayed the Sinner's Prayer. I received Christ."

Cathy was obviously using words strange to her usual vocabulary: "Sinner's Prayer" and "I received Christ." I was truly thrilled and delighted. "Oh, Cathy, that's great. That's wonderful!" I said to my friend.

With a serious look on her face, Cathy placed her hands flat on the table, leaned in toward me, and stared directly into my face. She asked with genuine wonderment, "Why didn't you tell me?"

The question plunged a dagger into my heart. Even now, I flinch. I had nothing to say. Nothing except "I'm sorry."

She said, "That's okay," or something like that, and we proceeded to talk. But her question haunts me, "Why didn't you tell me?" Why? I suppose I was waiting. Waiting for the right opportunity. Waiting until I thought she might be receptive. I never hid my faith, but neither did I want to push it onto someone else. Not even on a friend.

It is interesting to me that Cathy came to me, knowing I was a believer, wanting me to help her. Her coworker had the gift of evangelism, without a doubt, but now Cathy needed discipleship, and I was able to assist her. She wanted to start studying the Bible right away. So I volunteered to lead a study group, and we invited all the women from our Lamaze group. At the first session, one of the other women said, "You know, even during those years I went to that little Baptist Sunday school, I don't think I ever did that—received Christ, I mean." I said to myself, *If you don't take this opportunity, something is wrong!* After the others left, Cathy and I privately prayed with her to accept the Lord.

Cathy and I remain very dear friends. In fact, just the other day as we talked on the phone, she said, "You know, it's been ten years since I was baptized." Her daughter is now a believer and her husband, too, has been baptized. Several others within that original Lamaze group have become Christians.

I strongly believe in friendship evangelism. I think it's the way to win the world to Christ. But people are not brought into the kingdom just by my being their friend. At some point, I have to be specific with them and say, "I think you need Jesus."

The Story Goes On

As Nancy correctly surmised, Margaret exercises the gift of evangelism. She rarely misses the opportunity to interject Christ into any situation. Her integral love for Jesus is expressed in all areas of her life, including her real estate dealings and her relationships with coworkers.

All who know Nancy agree that she is gifted in teaching and maintaining long-term relationships. Her maturity draws women who need advice and comfort. But, still, Cathy's question, "Why didn't you tell me?" broadened her awareness of how easily we can build borders and, even unintentionally, limit ourselves to areas of personal comfortableness. Nancy faithfully shared about Jesus. Margaret shared *Him*. Sisters can learn about their specific gifts and develop them. But let us never be afraid to venture forth and speak directly of Christ. We all need the goal of evangelism, if not the gift.

Who in your life, in your circle of friends, in your neighborhood or "Lamaze group" is waiting? Waiting to hear the questions, "Would you like to know Christ? Do you want to pray?" Is it time to complement your silent, witness-by-example mode of evangelism with an assertive and specific invitation to faith? A sister may be waiting to hear it.

13

Addictions:
Letting Go
of False Images

———————

*"God doesn't make us wait until we are
completely healed to give away what we
have been given. God calls us to give away
healing and recovery immediately."*

    I met Becky soon after her high school graduation. She was a plump teenager with a cheerful disposition and confident manner. It was easy to assume that her passion and determination would ensure her success as an adult, no matter what profession or course she chose.

    Several years later, Jim and I attended an evening concert in our church. Afterward, our friend David introduced us to his date Rebecca. She was a beauty with raven black hair, porcelain white skin, luminous green eyes, and brilliant red lips. She was delicately thin, elegantly dressed, and of regal stature. As we shook hands and greeted one another, she smiled and said, "You don't remember me, do you?"

Quite truthfully, I did not. "I'm Becky," she announced. I was flabbergasted. She definitely had lost her baby fat. She was now an exquisitely beautiful woman.

David and Rebecca were soon married, and the friendship among the four of us flourished. Together we celebrated graduations, promotions, new homes, and babies. Together we grieved unemployment, miscarriages, and financial crises. Rebecca's style was dramatic, grandiose, and passionate. She did not just enter a room; she blew in and captured it. She was lively, animated, and emotional. For years, we teased her about getting on her soapbox. When we gathered for holiday meals and special occasions, her eyes welled with tears and her voice choked with emotion as she announced, "*This* is community." How she loved it.

October 4 is an important day in our four lives, for on that day one year, Rebecca and I each were admitted into hospitals: I, to give birth to my son; she, to fight for her life.

Rebecca's Story

I struggled with compulsive overeating since the eighth grade. I never had a normal breakfast, lunch, and dinner association with food. Mine was always a love/hate relationship. My mom took me to various doctors who always offered the same advice: Go on a diet. I was on and off diets throughout high school and college. I knew I had a weird food impulse, but I didn't know to call it an obsession. I didn't understand why I would panic and want to eat three doughnuts; I didn't understand how I allowed food to mask and numb my feelings.

The summer after college graduation, I started an intense physical workout program. Every morning I exercised at the YMCA and tried to eat low-fat, healthy food. I still gained weight because I was still overeating. A diet clinic was one thing I hadn't tried yet. *Here's something new,* I thought. The clinic prescribed diet pills and gave me shots, and within a few months I dropped down to 100 pounds. I was suspicious of the addictive side effects but managed to operate in denial. Pills and shots became my secret. I thought, *I'll do this for a little while and lose the weight.* I believed I was in control.

In the fall, I began my graduate studies at Fuller Seminary, working toward a Master of Divinity with an emphasis in marriage, family, and child therapy. I also began a part-time career as a print and runway model for petites. The following summer, David and I married. Life was fabulous. For the first time since early childhood, I was truly skinny. The amphetamines gave me the feeling that I had all the energy in the world and that I could achieve anything. I ate only one meal per day. I looked in the mirror and my self-esteem soared. I thought I had finally hit perfection.

Attached to this perfection was a string. A chain, really. An inner truth, a voice of denial, whispered, "You haven't achieved this on your own." My self-esteem was false.

For five years I deceived myself and convinced everyone around me that I was okay. I justified my addiction by telling myself I needed help given my grueling schedule and important studies. I even deceived the clinic. Over the years, my chart remained closed and unchecked. I somehow slipped in and out of the clinic, befriended the nurses, and my prescriptions kept getting refilled, even though at 5'3" I weighed just above 90 pounds. Finally a doctor caught up with me, read my chart, and announced, "You have achieved your goal weight and you need to wean yourself from the pills."

Absolute terror struck. Those tiny green tablets were my control, my superiority. They were my power. My mind knew I should relinquish the pills, but my body demanded them. In desperation, I found a psychotherapist. I cried so hard during my first session I could barely see. I felt ashamed of telling someone my secret. It took a year to wean myself from the pills, and not without great fear. When I graduated in the spring, I was clean. I had gained only nine pounds and thought I would be okay but, still, shame over my addiction permeated my self-esteem.

As a graduation celebration, David and I went to Europe with a study group from our church. When we returned, I fell into extreme depression and began to binge. My daily schedule and lifestyle at seminary were driven by *hurry, hurry, go as fast as possible*. I always carried more than a full load of classes, and I maintained a modeling career. Now my hectic pace hit a wall. I couldn't work full time as a counselor because of my lack of experience. I was bored. I tried to eat my way out of my depression. I ate bowl after bowl after bowl of sweet cereals. I filled myself with sugar and shame. I declined modeling sessions because in three months I gained forty-five pounds.

Compounding all this was misuse of my thyroid medication. I thought that if I took more, my metabolism would speed up and I wouldn't gain as much weight. My thinking was illogical and certainly irrational.

David was the only person aware of my addiction. When,

years earlier, my mother accidently found pills in my kitchen, I deceived her by swearing I wasn't abusing them and that I was under control. Now that I was off the pills, David watched me struggle. The confident, grandiose woman he married was insecure and inhibited. David was frustrated. If he bought food in an attempt to appease my cravings, he contributed to my bingeing. If he refused, I accused him of not caring about me. He felt helpless to help me. One night, as we lay together on our bed, my heart pounded nearly out of my chest because of my deliberate thyroid medication overdose. David started to cry; he could "smell death on me," he said. He was afraid I was going to die. His confession probably saved my life. I knew I had hit bottom and his fear motivated change.

The next morning, I called an eating disorder unit. One week later, on October 4, I entered the clinic as an in-patient for a six-week program. David stayed with me three nights a week and on weekends attended group therapy with me. Six weeks later, I was released to begin three months of aftercare. My struggle with food continued and I gained even more weight. One of David's coworkers saw me in a store and gushed, "I didn't know you were pregnant!" I wasn't. Only, everyone expected to see me around ninety pounds. My pain, shame, and helplessness were horrible.

During my six weeks of inpatient therapy, I learned I used food to handle my feelings. I am a very emotion-oriented person. During graduate school, the rush from the amphetamines made me feel what I call "super-adequate." After I completed school, I felt "inadequate." I didn't know how to feel simply adequate. Not knowing how to feel equal to people, I either felt superior or inferior. If you were skinny or smart, I felt less adequate than you. If I were skinnier or smarter than you, I felt superior. My self-esteem was entirely regulated by my weight, my size, what the scale said, and a comparison of my abilities to those of others. The armoire in my bedroom was a virtual symbol of my life. The outside was beautiful and orderly. Opening the doors revealed a chaotic mess of clothes, books, and papers. I worked to look perfect on the outside because the inside of me was a jumbled mess.

Life confronted me in two ways. I had to break out of the circles of "better than you" or "less than you." Then I had to come to terms with my relationship with food. I knew I had to get in touch with the God-given adequacy inside me. I started by putting little sticky papers on my steering wheel in the car that said, "I am adequate." I tried to breathe in this truth. "Christ died for me; I am created in the image of God."

Inside, very slowly, very quietly, change came. Inside first, then outside change followed. When the inside changed, destructive behavior stopped. David, too, had to change. He had to learn to say nothing about my food or my weight. He had to learn to feel his own feelings and stop being obsessed with mine. He had to stop taking care of me if I was to learn to care for myself.

Every week I met with Althea, my psychotherapist. She was calm and quiet and believed in me. She was a true sister. She taught me how to feel adequate around other women. Consciously and unconsciously, I tried to turn our sessions into the "better than/less than" game, but she wouldn't play. This happened in the late '80s, and her hair was still tightly permed. When I teased her and told her to "get current," she smiled and remained silent. When I compared her Ph.D., reputation as a theorist, and her professional psychotherapy career to my own vocational achievements, I felt inadequate. When I recognized what I was doing and put names to my behavior, I began to understand it.

I remember once in the hospital a nurse said to me, "God don't make no junk." I couldn't internalize that. I had to experience it in a relationship, in a sister. Althea believed in me and in my adequacy until I could finally believe in myself. In her, I saw Christ sitting across from me, saying, "You know, Rebecca, you can do all the dances in the world, and I still believe in you. You don't need to impress Me because I already love you." For almost four years, Althea represented Christ to me.

Slowly I improved, and final proof of my progress came with the news that I was pregnant. It was wonderful to be fat and for the first time have a great excuse! I knew I could deal with this transition in my body. I became baby-centered, not self-centered. For the first time, my tummy stuck out and I was proud.

During my pregnancy, I made conscious decisions about what, and when, to eat. I attempted to properly feed myself and my developing child. For the first time I didn't feel powerless or out of control with food. After my daughter Austin's birth, I continued to eat well for nursing. I was more concerned with her nutrition than with my desire to lose weight. When I stopped nursing, more of my extra weight came off. What was left was my body, and the body I had to accept.

The impulse toward food will be with me for the rest of my life. I may always stand between the choice of food for comfort or making a phone call to a friend for comfort. I'm much better now at going outside myself and trusting friends to be there with me.

Recovering from an addiction is all about death and resurrection. You have to let go. I had to release the food and pills, the grandiosity, the super-adequacy, along with my feelings of inadequacy, weakness, and helplessness. I had to let go of an image of myself at ninety-five pounds. For me, this meant trusting enough to let God's intended image be unveiled and revealed in me.

I have learned that it's through our own suffering and our own wounds that others are healed. Usually we hesitate to tell our personal struggles because we feel embarrassed and ashamed, or we feel inadequate. But it's our own woundedness, that place where Christ entered, that we use to help another. Yes, because I'm a skilled therapist, I can help clients reach wholeness. But with some clients, it's because of my own wounds that the healing happens. I love the Scripture "by His stripes we are healed" (Isa. 53:5 NKJV). My healed stripes are exactly what Christ uses for others.

James 5:16 says, "Confess your sins to each other and pray for each other so that you may be healed." This confession obviously requires relationship. Part of my own repentance and restoration occurred by making a commitment to the church and resuming regular worship, and going forward for prayers, anointing of oil, and laying on of hands. I had to confess my sin of truly hurting David and others through my eating disorder. But the real journey began by confessing the sin of hurting myself. God felt the pain and suffering along with me and enabled the process of forgiving myself.

God calls us to wholeness, but wholeness seldom happens overnight; it's a long journey for nearly all of us.

When we truly accept and completely give our lives to Christ as our Lord and Savior, God is not outside of us. We find Him inside. The wonderful but potentially frightening part of this is that as you go inward to find Christ, you find yourself at the same time. By fully knowing Christ, we move toward fully knowing ourselves.

I encourage others in recovery to ask for prayer in the church, to submit to the laying on of hands and anointing with oil. It's healthy to admit to the church our problems and our progress. Healing begins with becoming adequate enough to say, "I am weak, but I'm becoming stronger."

Sisters can help by saying, "It's really good seeing you" or "I'm happy to be with you again" rather than commenting on your appearance. Prayer is also something sisters can do for one another. Prayer is valuable to the woman in recovery. Since so many celebrations and gatherings center around food, ask your sister what foods are acceptable. Or if she would rather skip food, meet in a lovely garden or on a walking track.

These words helped me summarize my progress:

To create newness, you have to cover the soul and let grace rise. You must come to the place where there's nothing to do but brood, as God brooded over the deep, and pray and be still and trust that the holiness that ferments the galaxies is working in you, too. Only wait.

And somehow the transformation you knew would never come, that impossible plumping of fresh life and revelation, does come. It manifests itself in unseen slowness. So it would happen to me and so it will happen to all who set out to knead their pain and wounds, their hopes and hunger, into bread. Waiting is the yeasting of the human soul. . . . How did we ever get the idea that God would supply us on demand with quick fixes, that God is merely a rescuer and not a midwife?[11]

God's work is still being done in me. The yeast of change still rises.

The Story Goes On

David arrived alone at the hospital to meet our new son Taylor the day he was born. When Jim and I asked where Rebecca was, he replied, "In the hospital." We were sad, but not surprised. Her unraveling, her fraying, had become more and more evident in recent months.

I was not an example of a good sister in the weeks after Rebecca was released. I did not understand her struggle with food or why she couldn't control herself. However, the greater misunderstanding on my part was how to help her. In spite of my impatience, as months and even years went by, Rebecca taught me how to help her in practical, common-sense ways. On Friday evenings our two families traditionally met in one of our homes for dinner together. We learned how to prepare healthy, fat-free food. We served sugar-free drinks. With just a little effort, we assisted Rebecca's chances for recovery. The problem that once dominated every conversation is, these days, rarely addressed.

Rebecca's flamboyance and confidence returned without

the boost of amphetamines. Her vibrant enthusiasm for life is based on a foundation of solid stability and personal security. I am grateful our friendship survived in spite of my initial reluctance to acknowledge her trial.

Now, years later, Rebecca is a licensed therapist with a specialty in eating disorders. She is amazed that God doesn't make us wait until we are completely healed to give away what we have been given. God calls us to give away healing and recovery immediately.

Recently, she lent a measure of her hard-earned insight and wisdom to our friend Dawn. It happened that Jim and I attended an annual leadership retreat where everyone in the group briefly recapped the twelve months since we last met. When Dawn spoke, it was obvious that she was under severe stress. Astonishingly beautiful and an extremely talented singer, Dawn's words and body language suggested that she might be on the verge of an emotional breakdown. The rambling, distracted woman before us was not the Dawn we knew and loved. When she and I spoke privately later in the evening, I felt a vague reminder that I had witnessed this behavior before. When she said she felt inadequate, I knew from whom and where—Rebecca.

I asked for Dawn's permission to call Rebecca on her behalf. She agreed. After briefly describing Dawn's present state, Rebecca asked to speak to her. I do not know what Rebecca said, but Dawn softened physically and calmed as she listened. The very next morning, Rebecca and Dawn met. They continued to meet on a daily basis until the crisis passed. At this writing, they continue their counselor-client relationship and, for the sake of others, have given me permission to tell their stories.

When I saw Dawn's need, my immediate reaction was to call Rebecca. I *knew* Rebecca could help her. My job was not to try to fix or help Dawn myself, but to deliver her to Rebecca's arms. Then I had to let go and trust my sisters to each other's care.

It's very lonely to bring the mess of our lives and drop it at Jesus' feet by ourselves. It's much easier when someone helps us. Rebecca let go of a mess because David said, "I'm afraid." Dawn let go because I asked, "Can I call a counselor for you?" In both instances, someone said, "You're valuable enough to fight for." Someone said, "I love you and I don't want you to die. I want you to get help." That's the right motivation for the start of a long, hard journey back to wholeness. What a tragedy when no one is there to say that. That silence describes true loneliness.

Because Rebecca survived, Dawn has hope for herself. Isn't the exchange of hope the essence of being a sister?

Life will be brighter than noonday, and darkness will become like morning. You will be secure, because there is hope.

JOB 11:17–18

14

Weight:
Resolute or Unrealistic

------

*"My goal is to be as happy
with my body as I am
with myself."*

Babbie Mason is a much-admired singer and songwriter of contemporary Christian music. Her candid story reveals her frustration with fluctuating weight and stirs the issue of why women often feel they need to change to be good enough. Good enough for what?

At the heart of Babbie's story lies the question of why so many women invite defeat by comparing themselves to others. For Babbie, the comparison occurs with weight. Our society has abandoned the seventeenth century's idea that body fat indicated prosperity and health and, in many ways, that's unfortunate. Now many American women struggle for unrealistic slenderness.

Babbie's Story

A few years ago, on the first Sunday of the New Year, I was singing in a church near my home in Atlanta. The preacher welcomed us all and then encouraged us to stand and share our New Year's resolutions with the person next to us.

The lady I met said, "I resolved to lose the weight I gained during my pregnancy."

I commended her and asked, "How old is your baby?"

"Five weeks," she replied. Then she asked about my resolution.

I said, "Well, I, too, resolved to lose the weight I gained during my pregnancy."

She said, with great excitement, "That's great! How old is your baby?"

"Five years," I sighed.

Ever since I can remember, I have struggled with my weight. My mom called me "pleasingly plump." My neighbor called me "little fat gal." My father was a Baptist pastor, and some of my fondest childhood memories center around church traditions and celebrations: Homecoming, the Pastor's Anniversary, the Senior Choir's Annual Day. The entire church anticipated the arrival of guests from miles around to join us. Sunday afternoon, after the morning service and before the evening service, a feast was laid out. The pastor's family was seated at a special table, surrounded by the choicest delicacies, prepared by the church's best cooks. Now that I am reminiscing, I remember that each first Sunday of the month was a tradition to celebrate because our family was invited to a scrumptious Sunday dinner in the home of one of these fine cooks. I can't miss this opportunity to say that my own mother was the best cook of them all. Anniversaries, homecomings, first Sundays, and my mom's table all announced celebration. Celebration meant food. Food is still what I associate with home, comfort, and family.

The connection of food and celebration has been carried into my adult life. As a gospel artist, I'm famished after singing for two hours and meeting and greeting for a few hours after the concert. If I feel the concert was successful (and most of the time, I do), then I celebrate! When I first began as a songwriter, I would celebrate when someone besides my mother loved one of my songs enough to record it on his or her album. Even now, after I've been out on the road, eating too many meals out of a paper bag with a plastic fork, I return home and go straight to my kitchen to cook one of those meals I had as a child. Life on the road, an album cut here, and a song published there began to manifest itself as an extra pound here and a larger dress size there. Year after year, I have repeated the same "lose weight" New Year's resolution. But somehow, after two or three weeks, I'd go off the diet—again.

In my lifelong battle to subdue hips, waist, and thighs, I've learned to hide them, drape them, layer them, put elastic around them, belt them, disguise them, camouflage them, make them up, and color-analyze them. Whatever I do, they are still there! Now I decided to accept the fact that I have a weight problem and, with God's help, to deal with it. That decision is much easier said than done. Dealing with my weight isn't always easy.

Both pounds and pressure add up so I tend to be hard on

myself, comparing myself to others. I forget that a woman's physical appearance is only one factor contributing to her entire being. The emphasis on appearance causes many women to spend more time tending their bodies than their character. Acquiring the current shades of makeup, popular clothing labels, and the latest hairstyles seem more important than developing patience, kindness, or compassion. I need constant reminders (maybe we all need reminding) that a woman's inward character enhances her outward appearance. Her personality, her love of God, and her security in Christ, combined with her physical features, make her genuinely beautiful.

Losing weight is a journey, a process, for me. My goal is not to be thin. I have no desire to be a size eight. At my height, if I were a size eight, I wouldn't feel very well, and I probably wouldn't look very good either. My goal is to be as happy with my body as I am with myself. While walking this journey (I'm not a jogger), I've asked God to help me not retreat from life. My desire is to enjoy life to the fullest.

Recently, I was invited to Hawaii to sing for a conference. I asked a dear friend to go with me. For weeks before the trip, we planned all that we would see and do. She couldn't wait to go snorkeling in those emerald green waters. She said to me, "Now, we will have to get just the right kind of snorkeling gear. We can feed the fish out of our hands. And we can take pictures of everything!"

I said to myself, *Wait one minute. We won't do anything. I am not putting this body in a swimsuit. Why, I haven't been in a swimsuit since seventh grade gym. And I have no desire to capture the whole thing on film. Film is forever.* I began talking myself out of one of the most fun experiences on one of God's most beautiful beaches. All because I was afraid of what others might think about this body in a swimsuit. Then I said to myself, *Enough! You will go and buy a swimsuit. You will go snorkeling. And you will have a great time.* And I did! And I have the pictures to prove it. While I was on that beach, I saw bodies of all shapes, sizes, ages, and colors. I fit right in.

How true is 1 Samuel 16:7 (NRSV): "For the LORD does not see as mortals see; they look on the outward appearance, but the LORD looks on the heart." If we are true imitators of God, we will focus on the heart of a person, not his or her external wrappings.

I wish I could say I have mastered my weight problem, but I haven't. I wish I could truthfully say, "It's all right." It's not. However, in all my battles, bulges, and failed diet plans, there is God. He loves me! He does not change His mind about me because I fail to stay on a diet or I gain yet another pound. He cares about me and knows my inner thoughts. He knows my intentions and my resolutions. Importantly, He knows I need balance, routine, and discipline in my life. He knows I need help—help from someone who will hold me accountable, yet encourage me and cheer me on. I need a sister.

Not long after realizing this, I prayed for someone to assist me in the ongoing quest toward a suitable weight. Soon after, a friend and I met together after a Wednesday night worship service. As we stood together, she mentioned her desire to start a ministry as a personal fitness trainer and offer special assistance to interested women. Debbie was already teaching group aerobics at our church's activities center. Instantly, I knew the Lord had sent her to me. Standing right there in the aisle of my church was my answer to prayer! Now, three times a week, Debbie meets me at the church to help me tone, stretch, flex, pump, and sweat. She's my no-nonsense, lift-those-knees, former Army sergeant, God-sent!

With His inspiration, Debbie's motivation, and my perspiration, I approach a victory in my own Battle of the Bulge. I may have to fight this out on a daily basis, but by His grace, and with the encouragement of a Christian sister, I am encouraged to keep at it. I am continually thankful to be a recipient of the Lord's unfailing love and grace, which are constantly and consistently applied to my life. Through thick or thin (literally!), it's good to know I don't have to have a perfect figure to be loved by a perfect God.

By the telling of my story, you probably understand why I just love this verse: "This is what the LORD says to you: 'Do not be afraid or discouraged. . . . For the battle is not yours, but God's'" (2 Chron. 20:15).

The Story Goes On

How often do we, like Babbie, compare nearly everything—our bodies, our possessions, or our achievements—to those of others? Why do we feel the need to measure our personal accomplishments against the successes of those we love? Why do we compete with one another in areas that do not require it? Does it really matter who has the frizziest hair, weakest nails, biggest bra, or smallest jeans? Do babies really care who among them speaks, walks, or gets potty-trained *first*? Is it not time to distinguish between things significant and insignificant?

Is it possible that competitive conversations among women signal a need to feel accepted or exceptional? Are we looking for approval or for affirmation? Is boasting only a form of self-appraisal, a way of someone saying you're doing a good job—even if that someone is you?

Like Babbie, each of us needs to come to the place where we are determined to live life fully, abundantly, regardless of self-applied, limiting excuses like, "I'm too fat, too poor, too uneducated, too inexperienced."

Probably no one wants to be average. We all hope to be special. We are special. If we can absorb enough of this truth to fill the core of our souls, we can relax anxious eyes that look at every woman as potentially our superior. We would finish judging ourselves less than excellent on the basis of accomplishments, bank accounts, or body weight. Jesus "loves us as we are and not as we should be, [He loves us] beyond worthiness and unworthiness, beyond fidelity and infidelity, [He] loves us in the morning sun and the evening rain without caution, regret, boundary, limit or breaking point."[12]

When you read the following song lyrics, can you believe them for yourself? Can you help a sister who needs to believe this wonderful truth?

Just the Way You Are

You're too tall, you're too small
You're too much or not enough at all
You lash out, you shrink in
Oh where to begin

You're too brown, you're too round
You're too loose or maybe too much going down
You're too square, you're not free
But who do you see

In the mirror, mirror
Imagetaker
Can't you see the Image Maker?

Chorus:
No matter what they tell you
Shine like a morning star
Don't dare replace reflections
I like you just the way you are

You're unveiled, you're unplanned
You're unloved by impassive hands
No words left to say
What you feel this day

I wish you may
I wish you might
Know real love can make it right[13]

15

Mentoring:
When We Need a Tug of Faithfulness

"She releases me from the unobtainable goal of perfection and pushes me toward the attainable goal of excellence."

In many of the previous stories, women are greatly helped by other women. I identify with those who are grateful and thankful for friends ready to be true sisters. But there is yet another realm for women, one very much needed in our stressed and troubled world. Mentoring.

Barbara Pine is an author, speaker, and theologian. As a friend and sister, she encouraged me to collect women's stories, to refine my writing skills, to pursue my dream of writing a book. When she read my earliest work, she responded more with cheerleading than critiquing. When this book became a reality and I needed advice, I asked for more than her friendship. I asked for her to be my mentor.

I had no idea what I was asking. She took the role quite seriously. Her red ink slashed across my pages, cutting, editing, probing, questioning. She refused to supply all my answers. I had to think; I had to write. Her cheerleading was still there—just in a quieter voice.

She does not limit her mentoring to my writing. She drags me outside on cold, clear nights to find constellations and planets in the sky, modeling for me the joy of knowledge. She does not hide her own sorrows and losses but allows me entrance into the sanctuary of her heart. She is generous with her words and actions and time. She releases me from the unobtainable goal of perfection and pushes me toward the attainable goal of excellence.

The dictionary says a mentor is a wise and trusted counselor or teacher, but it doesn't talk about laughter and tears. A mentored woman seeks perspective, wisdom, and counsel. She expects discipline, correction, and an occasional setting straight. She knows the one who guides her aims her toward higher goals and greater development than she can approach alone.

But a true mentor cannot fill her role without a loving attitude and a basic belief in the one with whom she works. As I began constructing this chapter, I called Barbara for some ideas and direction.

"Give me about two minutes," she replied and pushed her own manuscript aside, willing to talk about mine. With her attention fully directed toward me, she asked, "So, what do you think about mentoring?"

Right there is the mark of a good mentor. *I* wanted to ask *her* the question. But she asked it of me, stretching me, making me find the right words. I fumbled, trying to explain why this book is important to me and why mentoring is. I know that every woman, if she lives long enough, will eventually run into sin and sorrow. For some, the collision occurs far too early, when the sweetness of childhood is knocked out of them by harmful adults. Most of us learn much later that even if the cause of our sorrow or failure makes sense, it still delivers quite a punch. Some of us will find ourselves at life's intersections not knowing which way to go. In all these places, a mentor makes an enormous difference. In my reply, I said something like that.

"How?" asked Barbara. "How does it make a difference?"

I shuddered at her question. I knew she was in her mentor role and this would be an intelligent discussion. But then she asked another question: "Can a sister be a mentor?"

I had to think on that one. This entire book has been focused on sisterhood, on encouraging women to come alongside another for comfort and support. A mentored relationship seems to take another step. "I think," I hesitantly replied, "that one woman may be both sister and mentor, but the roles are not the same. What do you think?"

"Sisters do all that they do for one another as equals," Barb began to clarify. "But once a sister becomes a mentor, the balance is no longer equal. A mentor becomes a teacher, which implies that the mentor knows more, at least about some things, than the mentored. My mentor . . ."

"What?" I interjected. "*You* have a mentor?" The silence on the line between us roared with meaning. Neither of us knew what to say.

I was surprised that Barb had a mentor; I thought she knew everything and always had. To me, she is all I want to be when I grow up. Barbara was surprised I felt that way. She knows how much she still needs to learn, how frequently her mind needs challenging. She said she was pretty sure that was clear to everyone who knew her. It wasn't clear to me. It took some persuasive talking on my part to convince her, as *my* mentor, to tell why *she* has a mentor.

Barbara's Story

Just this week, I received a letter from an editor who managed to bruise my ego. To receive some sympathy, I called my friend Nancy, who is a psychologist and who is what I call an emotion-mentor. She listened to me read the editor's opinion, and she listened to my reactions. She disagreed with my interpretation of it, but did so gently. That is, she was initially gentle. She listened patiently at first. She challenged my cerebral approach with good psychological questions like, "How does it make you feel?" As I grew stubborn and defensive, I heard the chin strap of her mentor's helmet snap shut.

With great deliberateness Nancy asked, "Do you really want to get into this? Are you ready to open it up?"

Nancy my mentor, not Nancy my sister, asked that question. She is skilled at backing me into any corners I'm foolish enough to create. As my mentor, she is a formidable opponent to my self-protecting sloppiness. My mind and emotions learn to dance in the ring, thanks to her education.

My experience has been that the mentoring of our spirit is quite a different thing. When I finished seminary, I left carrying a bruised belief system. Not because seminary spoiled my simple faith. Not at all. It was certitude and rigid practices outside the seminary that tore at my spirit. Simple faith, the currency of conservative Protestantism, is like a third parent to me. I was born to it. Only, by the time I reached my forties, it seemed as grievous to me as it was joyful, and I needed guidance. I needed help in being *me*. I wanted to follow Jesus, not the demands of Christian brothers and sisters who called for conformity as proof of genuine faith. I chafed at enforced style, and my resistance led to my being criticed.

In this case, a mature and brave Christian lent me wisdom and courage as I shared this particularly painful situation. I was prepared to speak for a group, but before I was approved, I was subjected to what might be called a cultural litmus test. I knew I would flunk. It was not a matter of biblical doctrine or a matter of historical orthodoxy. It was a matter of honesty getting me in trouble! My spiritual mentor gave me time to dab at tears and listened patiently.

"So," I asked, "if I get in trouble, will you hold my hand?" I guess I was prepared to hear an automatic "Of course!" but it didn't follow.

"No," came the answer.

"No" certainly wasn't what I expected.

"I do not need to hold your hand, Barbara. I will be standing by your side."

That is the mark of a mentor.

When Barbara finished her story, I had to wait for a moment before I could speak. "You do that for me," I told her gratefully. "Barb, that's what you do for *me*."

That is why mentoring is so important a subject to me and why I long for women to know it. Mentoring may sometimes be specialized or narrow in purpose. It does not always rise out of friendships. Barbara's spiritual mentor was a professor. The mentoring of Pastor Diane Reubel is another example of being mentored for a specific purpose.

Diane's Story

For seven years, Carla and I have maintained an intimate, but specific, relationship. We do not "do lunch." We don't attend movies or plays together. She is not what I would call a close friend. She is a valuable friend.

Our time together is not warm and cozy. It is directed and channeled. Once a month, I retreat to her home in west Seattle and, as much as anything, she gives me guided quiet time with God.

When I first went to Carla for help with what I call my "discerning process," I wanted to *know*, now, whether I was being called to ordained ministry. I wanted to move much too quickly. I said to Carla, "Here are the pieces. Put the puzzle together for me." That was my initial approach. However, her "spiritual word" *that* day to me was "Whoa!"

Carla taught me how to listen. To listen to God speak to me and to listen beyond my self-interests. Shutting my mouth and opening my ears was my first job in becoming a full-time minister of Jesus Christ. Thank goodness for my mentor's courage to say so.

The Story Goes On

In the second chapter of Titus, we read that "older women [are] to teach what is good . . . train the younger women" (vv. 3–4). As birthday after birthday rolls by and I approach that era known as middle age, I do not feel qualified to mentor. But my responsibility *is* to teach those around me. Whether I like it or not, other women, some younger and some older, observe my actions, hear my responses, and sense the attitude in my demeanor. At this age, knowing women are watching me, I long even more *for* mentoring as opposed *to* mentoring.

I know that it is my responsibility to reach back and grasp the hand of a sister, pulling her forward with me. But helping her scares me. What if I'm not strong enough to pull her on my own? What if I slip? But who takes my other hand, pulling *me* along and helping *me*?

Who tugs on me with perseverance and faithfulness? My mentor. When her strong, tight grip covers my hand, I am surprised by its strength. I am no longer afraid. I know I can make it and that together we can all reach the finish line of life.

These Are the Women We Come From

They are faces in photographs
Heads all held high
Not afraid to look life in the eye
They were women with backbone
Keepers of the flame
With a spirit even hard times couldn't tame

And I know this same blood is in me
And I meet their gaze one by one
Eyes strong and clear
I still feel them near

Chorus:
These are the women I come from
The faith that sustained them is bred in my bones
I know what I'm made of and where I belong
'Cause these are the women I come from

What did life bring them
What pain did they know
Stories the pictures didn't show
They were lovers of babies
And lovers of God
With lessons and laughter in their songs

Did they dream better dreams for their children
As they prayed silent prayers in the night
"Lord, make their way clear and always be near"

Now I have my own child beside me
And we gaze at them all one by one
Her eyes strong and clear
I draw her near, and say,

These are the women you come from
The faith that sustained them is bred in your bones
You know what you're made of and where you belong
'Cause these are the women
Survivors each one
They weren't always easy, but loving and strong
God's life force inside them is still going on
'Cause these are the women we come from[14]

16

Your Story
Goes Here

———

My house is quiet. The boys are sleeping; the dog is snug in her crate. Jim is under earphones, working on a piece of music. The moon is up, my writing is complete for the day, and I am enjoying solitude on the back deck.

Here, all is not quiet. I am soothed by the sustained note of the forest of trees rustling in the evening breeze. I hear the low timbral rumble of a distant frog. A responsive croak beneath the porch surprises me. A single cricket sounds, answered by a choir hidden in the darkness. This exchange of counterpoint and percussive pitch is accompanied by inter-mittent flashes from lightning bugs. Believe it or not, this orchestra of the night directs my thoughts to my sisters.

A call. A response. A solo cry. A chorus of answers. Every woman, without exception, needs to talk to someone. Every woman needs to hear a voice in return. Every woman has a story worth telling. And a story worth hearing. Your story goes here. Now, tell it.

For your sake. For Christ's sake. For the sake of your sisters. Tell it.

The Story Goes On

His voice was water to her soul
As she drank His words of hope
And it quenched her thirst
He told her all she's ever done
And she knew He was the one
The Savior of the earth
Then she ran, wanting others to believe
And said, "People, come and see—come
     and see."

Chorus:
And the story goes on
The weak are made strong
Each time it's told others find hope
And the story goes on.

We are all living proof
Of the power of truth
And one by one we pass it along
The story goes on.

We all have a story we can tell
Like the Woman at the Well
Whether great or small
And the chapters written in our hearts
May help someone through the dark
Or somehow break their fall

Cause His love finds its way into the night
Through the pages of our lives
Through our lives

Chorus:
And the story goes on
The weak are made strong
Each time it's told others find hope
And the story goes on.

We are all living proof
Of the power of truth
And one by one we pass it along
The story goes on.[15]

NOTES

1. Dick Tunney/Melodie Tunney © 1994 BMG Songs, Inc. (ASCAP), Dick and Mel Music. All Rights administered by BMG Songs, Inc. All rights reserved. Used by permission.

2. Richard J. Foster, *Prayer: Finding the Heart's True Home* (San Francisco: Harper Collins, 1992), 73.

3. Ann Dally, *Inventing Motherhood* (New York: Schocken Books, 1982), 47–48.

4. Bonnie Keen/Tori Taff/Darrell Brown © 1991 Myrrh Records, Meadowgreen Music, Julie Rose Music, Grey Ink Music and Tori Taff Music, ASCAP.

5. Oswald Chambers, *My Utmost for His Highest* (Nashville: Discovery House, 1992).

6. Philip Yancey, *Disappointment with God: Three Questions No One Asks Aloud* (Grand Rapids: Zondervan, 1988), 157.

7. Paula Carpenter/Susan Ashton/Gayla Borders © 1994 Birdwing Music/Song Tree Publishing Co., Inc., Birdwing Music admin. by EMI Christian Music Publishing. All rights reserved. Reprinted by permission.

8. Michael Puryear/Jeff Silvey/Cheryl Rogers © 1995 Birdwing Music (ASCAP)/Careers—BMG Music Publishing, Inc./ Final Four Music (BMI)/Word Music (ASCAP). Birdwing Music admin. by EMI Christian Music Publishing. All rights reserved. Used by permission.

9. Charles Stanley, *How to Listen to God* (Nashville: Thomas Nelson, 1985), 146.

10. Rachel Conrad Wahlberg, *Jesus According to a Woman* (New York: Paulist Press, 1975), 24–25.

11. Sue Monk Kidd, *When the Heart Waits* (New York: Harper & Row, 1990), 43, 28.

12. Brennan Manning, *The Signature of Jesus* (Old Tappan: Chosen Books, 1988), 126.

13. Becky Thurman/Geoff Thurman © 1994 P. E. Velvet Music (a div. of the Harding Music Group)/Seventh Son Music, Inc. (a div. of Glen Campbell Music Group) ASCAP. All rights reserved. Used by permission.

14. Bonnie Keen/Tori Taff © 1993 Julie Rose Music/Tori Taff Music, ASCAP. Used by permission.

15. Janice Chaffee/Ty Lacy/Connie Harrington © 1995 Word Music (a div. of Word Music) ASCAP/Shepherd's Fold Music (BMI) (admin. by EMI Christian Music Publishing)/Edward Grant, Inc. (admin. by Reunion Music Publishing) ASCAP. All rights reserved. Used by permission.

About the Author

Janice Chaffee has worked in the Christian music industry for eighteen years, presenting seminars nationally and internationally, as well as establishing and hosting an annual women's retreat in Estes Park, Colorado.

She is Executive Co-Producer of the albums *Sisters* and *Sisters: The Story Goes On*.

Janice currently lives in Nashville, Tennessee, with her husband and two sons.

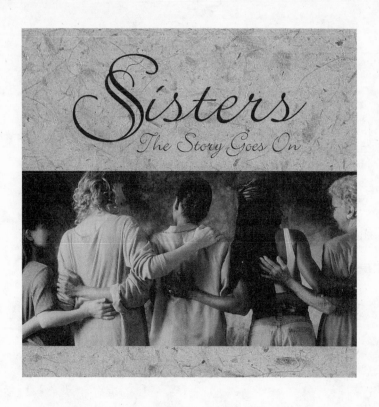

*Available at Christian Bookstores
everywhere on high quality cassettes
and compact discs*

WARNER
ALLIANCE